Daddy Loves His Girls

T. D. JAKES

Daddy Loves His Girls

CREATION HOUSE
BOOKS ABOUT SPIRIT-LED LIVING
ORLANDO, FLORIDA

Dedication

This book is dedicated to my wife, Serita, who has given me many years of love and companionship. Thank you, honey, for surrounding our marriage with five children whom I deeply love.

I dedicate this book to my daughters, Cora and Sarah, whom I want to publicly affirm as I already have written of my sons. I celebrate my daughters' uniqueness and giftings. I can see the strength and character of their grandmothers' and great-grandmothers' saturating them and fanning the flame in their eyes.

I know they will be tested and challenged, ostracized and confronted. Nevertheless, they will spring up again with all the buoyancy of the rich heritage from which they were proliferated and with hearts that dare to trust in God.

As they face the new horizons of the uncertain future, my heart is encouraged to know that behind their glistening smiles lie brilliant minds full of potential and bright with opportunity. Since I shall have whatever I say, I call them ladies of excellence. They will take on the challenges of life and conquer its limitations. I encourage them to be all they can be.

Live vivaciously, love deeply and pray fervently. Remember to give with simplicity and to serve with humility. Still, observe that meekness does not necessitate weakness. Therefore, when challenged by obstacles, fight with tenacity.

Finally, do not revel in your failures nor play in your past. Overcome every doubt, sign no treatise with the enemy and take no hostages. Never settle for less than your best or compromise your principles for your pleasures. And at last when the war is over, always remember to live off the spoils. Daddy loves his girls!

Contents

Chapter One

Daddy Loves His Girls

Dear Girls,

I am writing to you from the heart of your father, who
sees you as twinkling stars in the night. You glimmer in the
dark places, and you brighten my nights. I write to you to
tell you my perspectives on who you are. I write to you to
reaffirm that you are special and unique, each one beautiful
in your own uniqueness. You are always special to me,
never ordinary. This is my opportunity to share the relationship a father has with his growing daughters. I will tell you

about days you will not remember. I will speak of smiles and gurgling baby sounds you could never recall. These are moments etched into my mind forever. I will never forget them. You are beacons of light shining in the stormy days of my tempestuous youth.

My dear daughters, this is a tribute of life for you, a message that you will hear later and enjoy longer than I can stay around to watch. As your life continues may you always know your earthly father's thoughts and your heavenly Father's heart.

My daughters, though I write for you, this message explodes in my heart for all of the Father's daughters, every woman and every girl. So, dear reader, I invite you to listen as the Holy Spirit weaves a warming blanket under which all may snuggle and be blessed. This is a rare opportunity to examine the inner channels of the Father's heart.

I also write on behalf of every father who ever heard the sound of his daughter's voice erupting into that harmonious blend of pitch and praise, as she gleefully greets him at the door, saying, "D-a-d-d-y!" I never knew one word could have so many syllables. It is the sound of rushing waters gushing across rocks in a stream deep in the mountains. It is the wondrous dynamics of an expectant heart that seeks little and gives much.

My daughters, my girls, what a gift you are to me. Thank God, He let me know you and nurture you! You should never feel unloved or unwanted, for you are the fountains of your mother's youth running free, reminding us of who we were. You are the silky satin in my grandmother's finest handkerchief. You are my pulse; my blood warms your veins. You are my heart!

As I write these gleanings gathered from the harvest of my heart, perhaps in some small way they will reflect a fleeting glimpse of God's heart toward you. He is the everlasting Father of which men are just poor imitations. We are

flawed and cracked, our virtues paling in the brilliancy of God's divine character. Yet in some small caricature we may slightly trace His heart with trembling hands and broken crayons into some recognizable form of how much He loves His children and, particularly today, His girls. I am created in the image of God as a man and as a father. I love all my children equally, but I do not express love to each one the same way. In the same way, the God we serve loves His children, but perhaps, if I am at all like Him, He loves them equally but differently.

Anyone who knows anything about love at all will tell you that love cannot be copied, duplicated, repeated or forced. Each feeling is unique, just as the dripping colors of finger painting bear the uniqueness of the artist's own fingerprints. It is shaped into a moment and mood that could never be recaptured quite the same. Perhaps the daughters of Zion would stop their weeping if they knew how dear they were to their Father. Perhaps they would rise up out of the ashes and cast their fears to the wind if they knew that the Father assigns angels to their charge and gives such attention to details that He has numbered every strand of hair that caught in their combs.

It is a mother's privilege to carry in the warmth of her own body the squirming, wriggling embryo of life, a capsule of promise and a child of the future. She shares her own body heat, her food and the very air she breathes with a child that we as fathers cannot feel or feed. It is the mother's privilege to feel in her own womb the turning body of the child whose only blanket is her heated flesh. She lays her hand on her abdomen and speaks to the child she harbors and feeds within the chamber of her own loving space.

Fathers stand by, clumsily meandering along, assisting when we can, feeling a little foolish, perhaps a little left out. From morning sickness to mood swings, we can see the

effects of the baby, but like the wind we cannot see *it!* Our nervous pacing serves only to make tense the expectant mother as we both realize the nearness of birth and the greatness of responsibility. Your mother has carried you, my seed, in her pouch like a mother kangaroo, so you have done everything together with her before you were even born. You climbed steps together, ran and walked together, slept in the same bed and ate the same foods. You bonded!

But, before you excommunicate fathers from the festivities of parenthood, let me speak on our behalf. My wife carried you, but I waited for you. I was your first audience. Your first performance was for me. I beheld your first entrance. It was a grand entrance indeed. No distant waiting room for me. I waited right at the spot in the room like a catcher at home plate. I stood perched, waiting to see you come forth out of your dressing room into the light.

I remember a moment your mother couldn't see. Her strength had been expended in pushing, her hair disheveled and her body stretched wide. Her eyes were wide, her jaws filled with air, her legs gapped like the curtains opening to a Broadway play. The star was coming; the room was charged. I had to remind myself to breathe. She pushed; I coached. She labored; I encouraged. And then — ugh — it happened. She was without question the one who birthed you. But, little girl, when you first stepped on the stage, I saw you!

Peek-a-boo, I saw you, still easing your way from the pockets of birth into the mainstream of life. I saw your crown, you princess of potential, a goddess of grace. You were created in the image of the Lord Himself.

I will never forget that moment that you, my first daughter, were born, wide-eyed and gazing. Now, I know they say babies cannot see clearly, and maybe they can't see detail, but I could have sworn you were looking right at me. That blissful moment seemed to last at least a week.

Time got sucked into a vacuum; silence filled the room; tears came into my eyes. I had seen a miracle. I had seen God face to face.

You haven't lived until you have seen Him appear in the form of birth — miraculous. It reminds your heart of the great possibilities of new beginnings.

His handiwork was upon my seed. It was His work all right. His seal of authenticity was all over you. It seemed to me that the angels had patted your face and heaven was somewhere in your eyes. When I looked at you at that moment, God felt closer. When all had left the room and your precious mother, who had done the real work, was sound asleep, I just came where you were and watched over you. I will always do that. Wherever, whenever you need me, I'll be watching over you. They finally dragged me away from the window. Smiling deep within, I walked down the hall humming a soft song. I thought to myself as I hummed down the hall, "Peek-a-boo, little girl, I saw you!"

You cannot recall this moment, although you were center stage. But I will never forget it. I see it every time I look at you. I see it at every stage of your development — your eyes gazing at me, obviously intrigued by me. One look won me forever; you are mine. Wherever you go, whatever you do, you will always be mine. My seed is lost in you. I cannot retrieve it, erase it or deny it. You will always be my girl. Right or wrong, weak or strong, you are mine!

As ages and stages collide, and your hair increases while mine decreases, I reflect on the moments that you will never recall. It is that moment of birth that reaffirmed in my mind that I was needed. My protective nature was stimulated, my provisional instincts started wanting to provide. Whatever you needed I wanted you to have. Never doubt that the Father wants His daughters to be blessed! It is His joy to see you flourish and succeed.

Women who approach God nervously, uncertain of His response to their problem, may know motherhood, but let me share with you how strongly a father wants his daughters to be blessed. If you understood a father's heart for his little girl, you would run into your heavenly Father's arms gleefully. No matter what He is doing, He is glad to see you come, your eyes praising Him, looking at Him as if He could move heaven or hell. Don't you realize that your approaching Him is a praise all by itself?

> "So don't be afraid, little flock. For it gives your
> Father great happiness to give you the Kingdom"
> (Luke 12:32, TLB).

A real father is giving and generous. He is wise in that he will not give to the point of destruction. He doesn't want to damage the character of his child, but he longs, nevertheless, to bestow gifts lavishly. In fact, most men express love through giving. If you ask a man, Do you love me?, he will always make reference to what he gives you. The giving of things is one of the ways we men express affection and ascribe value. I realize that there are other gifts, such as time and attention, that to you may seem more beneficial. But remember, if a man is not dysfunctional or disadvantaged, he loves to give.

Giving opens for us an avenue of expressing affection without being encumbered with words. If you knew your Father's love, you would run to Him. He gets as much out of giving as you get from receiving.

It is sad to say that many girls will never experience firsthand the love of an earthly father. Somehow they have been denied the privilege of cultivating a wholesome relationship with their natural father. However, even they will recapture what they lost as they come to know their heavenly Father.

Do you know Him? I mean, really know Him? Or is He a

stranger, a foreign concept with no point of reference from your past to which He may attach Himself for definition? If you don't know your heavenly Father, you are missing a wonderful chance to touch a loving father. He is not irresponsible. Neither is He insensitive or selfish. Curl up in His arms, and I know you will be safe and secure from all alarms.

It is wonderful to realize that the Father stands ready to reveal His love in your life. He is the real Father whom the rest of us poorly imitate at best, and probably frustrate as we stumble through our machismo trying to achieve the gift of relationship! He is the reality of which I can only be abstract. But I hope, dear daughters, that in some way I will help to make it easier for you to perceive Him through this abstract attempt I have made to portray Him. If I have been a good father in any way, He is all of that and more. If I have failed, blame me — not Him. He never fails!

Shhh, here comes the pitter-patter of little feet and the gleam of the trusting eyes. The words fill the room: "Daddy, could you open this for me?" I clothe my response in my deepest, most masculine voice, filled with all of the gallantry of history: "Give it to me." I open the container as she gazes with wide eyes and obviously thinks, My daddy is so strong. I am her hero. When she is impressed, I feel strong and important, invincible and needed. I never knew I could get so much self-esteem out of a bottle of catsup!

We nourish each other. She gives me praise; I give her safety. She gives me adoration; I give her affection. Even the hardest of men melt when they give away this kind of affection. It can reduce the most conservative entrepreneur to crawling on the floor playing "horsie" and neighing with his head back as if he were a young colt. Even bigots smile at babies. They will smile at a baby and then not hire the father who needs a job so that he can feed the baby they just embraced.

It is the ultimate release for a man to enjoy the feminine heart without all of the hunting and conquest. Our ego is never threatened through this love. It is wholesome and holistic. It is like a deep breath of clean air. It fills us with fuel and eases the tension of tough days.

You see, darling, it is the love that makes it special. Your love is pure and unpretentious. It gives a man a love he can trust without intimidation or suspicion. No wonder Jesus said, "Unless you...become like children you shall not enter the kingdom of heaven" (Matt. 18:3, NAS). A child's love feels no threat of rejection, no fear of reprisal. It is born out of an unconditional appreciation of who we are. It is not laced with all the complications that come from erotic love. It is the love a man can have for a woman without the complexities of sexuality. Besides, it is so easy to impress someone who is so easily satisfied.

Today, I am her hero! That is what most men need, to feel like they are somebody's hero. In her eyes I am a knight in shining armor. She gets excited if I fix a bicycle. She gets worried if I scratch my hand. I am Superman without the blue tights. I am Captain America without the shield. What a feeling she emits from her wondrous eyes and smiling face. She believes in me. The feeling we fathers crave is the feeling that comes from knowing that someone affirms us and appreciates what we have to give. There is no fear of failure, no anxiety to perform or impress. There is just love!

You miss so much of God's power when you parade yourself as being self-sufficient. He longs to be your hero. He longs to open things you cannot open and move things you cannot move. He would do it for the gleam in your eye. He would do it just to hear your voice telling someone else how strong your Father is. He would do it just to express how deeply He is committed to your good! He has the power, and He longs to perform. He is greater

than earthly fathers. We make vows we don't keep and promises that we fail to accomplish, but not Him. He is able to perform at all times what He has promised in your life!

Now, daughter of mine, I understand that as years go by you will see cracks in my pottery and rust on my shiny suit of armor. Alas, you will realize that I am just a man. My angel wings will wilt and my faults will manifest and, eventually, as you look at me through the mature eyes of womanhood, you will find out that your hero was just a man. He has flaws and faults, cracks and crevices. Someday you will find out that there will be things I can't open and mountains I can't move. For that moment of disappointment I apologize in advance.

I wish I could be all that you see when you look at me through your little brown eyes. When you wake from your sleep like Dorothy in the land of Oz and find out that the wizard had a can opener in his pocket, I can only offer you Jesus. He is the original of which I am just a poor copy. Though it is true that I am poorly constructed and frail, I want you to know that my frailty is everywhere else but in my love for you. There I will always be a giant.

"What's love got to do with it?" one singer asks. Everything, I answer. For love is a guarantee that no matter what happens, I will always be around. Even if I am feeble and tremble like a willow and my skin hangs in leathery folds, I will be there. And when death comes and pulls me away from view and I can no longer communicate with you, just know these truths. I may not be where you can see me, but if there is any chance to look at you, whether from a cloud or a camcorder, here is my promise to you. No matter how you fail or falter, stumble or crawl, I will be there — somewhere — still gawking at you. Because you will always be daddy's girl.

This is my point. When I saw you I was already a man. I was mature. I understood some things that you may not

know. I knew you would fail. I knew you would stumble, and I knew that some of those failures would be painful for us both. When I loved you it was with the full knowledge that I was loving a clay pot. It was shaped into a doll and painted like a sunset, but it was still a clay pot, a human just like me. No matter, I still love you. You are my daughter! As you discover my humanity, you may be amazed. But I knew yours from the beginning. Never run from me. I already know who you are, and I will love you when all others forsake you. I will love you still.

This is a father's love. Do you realize that our Father loves you like that? He already knew you would fail and falter. He always knew you were human. He always knew that you would have struggles. No matter how well you were nurtured, there would still be areas that challenged you. He has sent me to tell you — even after all that has happened to you and with you and in you — that He has not changed His mind. He loves you still!

> The Lord hath appeared of old unto me, saying, Yea, I have loved thee with an everlasting love: therefore with lovingkindness have I drawn thee (Jer. 31:3, KJV).

In this world of broken homes and trembling relationships, it is important that we don't lose complete definition of a father's love. His strong arms pick you up when you are low. In those arms you nestle as he carries you to bed when sleep has claimed you on the couch. It is on his shoulder you weep when the tears can no longer be contained. His wisdom seems so sovereign, his compassion so pure. He is made for your protection. He is your father.

Chapter Two

You Are Not the Same

$\mathcal{I}$ have but two daughters, born eleven months apart. They are so close that people often thought they were twins, but not me. Even when my wife decked them out in the same lace-covered, pristine dresses complete with crinoline slips, and they beamed at me with their sun-filled smiles and shining eyes, I always could tell them apart. They are not the same. They may even dress alike occasionally, but they are quite different. They laugh together and play together, but they are as far apart as east is from west.

Isn't it good to be able to love someone without feeling like they must be just like you? There is neither a right nor a wrong, just different. Many people always feel that how they are is how everyone must be. They have appointed themselves as missionaries traveling to the rest of us to teach the natives to be more like them. Wrong. None of us is the same. Our thoughts are different. Our preferences are different. We are as diverse as we are multiple. For every person you see on this planet there is but one pattern. The world has never seen one of you before, and it will never see another one again!

You are unique, dear daughter. That is what makes you priceless. I could never, ever replace you. If I had a thousand more children, each one wonderful, none would be you! I will do all that I can to preserve your life because you are irreplaceable. Never give up your uniqueness to be what you admire in someone else. Glean all that you can from everyone, but duplicate none. You are too priceless as an original to be reduced to a cheap copy!

I noticed when my first daughter, Cora, was born that she was quiet and sedate. She is mild-mannered and shy. She is creative and talented but conservative and coy. Her quiet spirit fills a room with tranquility. Words are not needed. She is content with her own thoughts. Her mother is woven into her face like a fine thread woven into a garment. Her bright eyes only hint at what her pursed lips will not speak. She smiles; she laughs; she speaks. But the inner channels of her heart are locked behind a door that says, "Do not disturb!" She guards her thoughts from the brightness of public exposure, only occasionally calling a news conference with me to announce the need to discuss some weighty matter worthy of breaking the silence.

She became ill when she was a baby, still squirming in my arms. As we attended to her, she was almost too beautiful to look at, too special to describe. It was as if angels had

flapped their wings all over her face. Even now my words are intimidated by my feelings. Even a rich and full vocabulary cannot compete with the magnitude of a feeling. How can something so right go wrong? We associate sickness with darkness, dankness. Plagues and disease are ugly business. I was shocked to find out that beautiful people are not exempt from fighting ugly problems. My heart sank as the doctor told me to rush my daughter to the hospital.

I started to drive her home to her mother, who was by then pregnant with our second daughter. On my way I picked up my own mother for company — just to be present, not to talk. I was too preoccupied with my fear. As I drove, panic flooded my heart, and I tasted the acid-like sensation of fear in my mouth. My mother, who has always had the gift of looking into my face and seeing my heart, knew something was terribly wrong. I drove in a daze toward my home.

Finally, I broke the silence to share with my mother that the doctor had said I should put my daughter in the hospital that day! In the middle of my jumbled thoughts and suppressed tears, a thought leaped on the screen of my mind. I was amazed at the very notion. I, with bulging eyes, asked my mother a question that neither of us will ever forget. "Is this how you feel about me?" I blurted out. I never knew you could love anyone that much.

To think that my own mother and father might feel that way about me, and I didn't even know it! Oh, I knew that they loved me. But I mean this desperate, insane, pulsing feeling that made me feel like the sun would never shine without my child and all the grass would cease to grow if she were not all right. I confess, I was amazed. It is a different feeling from marital love, although marital love is stimulating and rich. Perhaps it is the reality that the baby is so helpless and vulnerable that makes this love feel different. Whatever it is, I could hardly drive down the road.

My pulse was racing, my temperature had escalated. I was more worried about that baby than I had ever been about anything in my whole life. No problem, no bill or anything else could outweigh the burden that I held in my arms as I drove to our home. That's right, I was so out of it I didn't even put you in the car seat. I held you in my arms. I was afraid to let you go!

To my pending question, the question that demanded that my mother define her feelings for me, she replied softly, "The way you feel about that child is the same way I feel about you." Suddenly, I knew the secret that only parents know. There is no word for it. You can only know it when you have your own child. It is the gift of love that God allows parents, or I should say good parents, to enjoy. It is as intoxicating as wine! You poor fathers who have willingly abandoned your children, I feel sorry for you. There is a level of love and fulfillment you can only know when you look into the face of your child! Find your child and love him or her. It will heal you both.

> That Christ may dwell in your hearts by faith; that ye, being rooted and grounded in love, may be able to comprehend with all saints what is the breadth, and length, and depth, and height; And to know the love of Christ, which passeth knowledge, that ye might be filled with all the fulness of God (Eph. 3:17-19, KJV).

To think that I was loved like that and didn't know it! The Bible says that the love of Christ passeth knowledge. It is like my daughter who will grow up and never know or remember that horrifying ride from the doctor's office. She will have difficulty comprehending how much I love her.

Have you yet realized how intensely God loves you? I mean, in spite of your afflictions, He loves you. Just as I was clutching my daughter, the Father is holding on to you.

He has held you through the rough places, trusting the strength of His arms to keep you through the pains of life. It has been a long ride, but He is still holding on.

When I think of the inevitable days when my dearest daughters may wonder if I love them, it saddens my heart. They will, perhaps, misjudge an action at a busy moment. Perhaps a harsh word will produce a torrent of tears and a deluge of doubt that makes them wonder if they are loved. Or maybe it will be something they thought I should have given them or a place I should have taken them. They will wonder, Does he love me? That is so sad. Because they will not remember the clutching fingers of a loving father who held them through the storm and the rain.

Perhaps you have asked the Father for something, and He didn't do what you thought He should. Perhaps you are disappointed that He didn't show up in the way you thought He would. Before you feel unloved, take a moment and think. Isn't there evidence in your life that from time to time He held you through the rough places and brought you through a storm? Don't you dare act as if the Father doesn't love you just because He doesn't always cater to you. Perhaps you should be glad for the love He has already shown and the night rides that He has already carried you through.

I will never forget that ride to the house. Perhaps one of my greatest fears was finding the words to tell my pregnant wife that our daughter had to go into the hospital. It was a horrifying message for me to deliver, partially because I have never been admitted to a hospital in my entire life, and partially because pain causes most men to regress into their second childhood. Not just pain but sickness — even a cold — can turn a 250-pound football player into a runny-nosed, sniffling little boy who wants his mother to bring some soup!

But the greatest fear was really based on the image I saw

when the doctor said *hospital*. It traumatized me because I had pictured my daughter, the one who normally would be riding Big Wheels in the park, hooked up to life-support systems with oxygen tubes in her nose. I was frantic with worry.

Worse still, I knew that as soon as my wife saw me she would see through any brave facade I could muster. She has some innate ability to see right through your eyes with an inborn X-ray machine. So when I came in the door, she was waiting. She has that gift that women have of asking a question but bypassing your words and running your face through some scanner to see if you are telling them everything.

I knew I couldn't pass her scanner. But I decided to try because I didn't want her to detect the depth of my concern. Since I usually handle crises fairly well, she would really be alarmed if I walked in the door and started screaming! (Which, incidentally, was what I wanted to do!)

I walked in the door with my baby and my mother. Three generations of strong, wonderful women were together, each one of them representing a different avenue of strength and love. I attempted to sound light and pleasant. I struggled to remember what I would normally say. So I said somewhat emptily, "Did anyone call me?" My wife disregarded the stupidity of the question, ran her scanner across my face and asked, "What's wrong with the baby?" I was busted!

"We've got to take her to the hospital," I blurted out with tears welling up in my eyes. The dam had just cracked, and there we were.

I will never forget how ridiculous we must have looked, with mother holding the baby and my wife and me holding each other as if we had been in a plane crash. Both of us were in tears; I mean, we were just howling. And the poor baby who needed to be taken to the hospital was looking

at us as if to say, "What's wrong with you?"

It was then that I knew beyond a shadow of a doubt that God heals. That's because if I were God and felt the way I felt I would have immediately healed my daughter. I would have touched her and healed her right on the spot. Do you need a healing? Ask God; He loves you like a father, and He cares how you feel. He is not some aloof, macho, egotistical God who has no compassion for His children. No, He loves you, and He wants to bless you now!

> If ye then, being evil, know how to give good gifts unto your children, how much more shall your Father which is in heaven give good things to them that ask him? (Matt. 7:11, KJV).

Although I couldn't heal her, God could, and she is fine today because her father turned her over to his Father! You see, I knew how much I loved her. I soon had to trust in the fact that He loved her more than I did. I realized that He could watch over her better than I. I decided to trust His decision. And Father to father we walked through that dark moment together! Oh, whatever you are facing, do not doubt what I am telling you. Daddy loves His girls.

Let me share the next miracle in my life with you, my daughters, and with you, the world. Just when I thought there was no more room in my heart, my new baby girl came. There should have been at least a one-hundred-piece marching band to announce Sarah's arrival. She was the complete opposite of the first. She was a doll baby. Her long, willowy body was sculpted and designed. Her bright eyes were accented by a toothless smile that would stop traffic. She was a perfect little lady, at least until she got hungry. It was then that this cherub, this love Cupid, turned into a creature from *Tales From the Crypt*. Doll baby could scream like Tarzan. She turned red in the face and literally intimidated everybody until she got what she wanted! She

had a temper that would arrest a train on the track!

I was in school. God wanted me to learn respect for differences. She may have looked like the other daughter, but she certainly wasn't her. This was an aggressive little girl who went after what she wanted with fire.

You see, our society has spent so much time criticizing differences that we fail to see God in diversity. He never made two leaves alike. He wants us to be different. Different doesn't mean less than or more than, just different. Have you ever despised your own uniqueness? Have you ever wished you were someone else? If you have, I arrest that spirit in Jesus' name. God made whom He wanted when He made you, and He has a purpose for your life. You are going to need those strengths and vulnerabilities He has carefully mixed together in you. You are going to need them to play your role in history. No one can do it but you. God used my girls to explain diversity to me.

My wife and I could not stereotype our children. Each one sent us back to our knees for direction. There are no recipes for rearing children. Each time, the recipe is altered by the change in the main ingredient. The only thing my wife and I knew for sure was that although they looked a little alike, these girls were not the same. My baby girl was fine as long as she got what she wanted. It wasn't that she was spoiled. She was assertive, and she remains that way today. She is high-spirited and tempestuous. She was soon climbing out of the baby bed as if it were a toy for her amusement. She was aggressive, to say the least!

She is strong-willed and relentless. Whatever God has planned for her, I suspect these tools will be essential. I have learned that her personality is a clone of my own. She is definitely the kind of girl who isn't afraid. There is little shyness in her. She will walk onto a stage before anybody, without fear. She is incredibly bold and confident. She is me, in a dress. Thank God, she has her mother's features, but she is filled with my tenacity. She is a spicy dish. Like Mexican cuisine, she is full of fire! Sarah, you are destined to be a wild woman full of faith and power. For even now you are a rope-jumping, leaping, laughing gust of wind. You are delightful, my daughter, through and through.

Each daughter will play a different part in history. They are not the same. They will be different. Did you know that God has never intended for you to be like anyone else? He wants you to be yourself.

I couldn't love my daughters any more than I do. Yet, they are completely different. The reason I love them is because I love them. It is not their mannerisms that I love. It is not their personalities alone but the person behind the personality. They are uniquely created and divinely endowed in Christ Jesus to perform differently.

Think a moment. If God hadn't made you as He did, you wouldn't have been able to persevere as you have. There are many people who couldn't take what you have been through. God wants to use you in a unique way to be a blessing to those around you. Remember, people are blessed when you are sincere. Not perfect, just genuine!

You have a part to play. Don't let anyone manipulate you into forsaking your own uniqueness. Those people weren't built for your life's destiny, and they can't play the role. Aren't you glad that God prepared you for life instead of preparing life for you? So, whether life is ready for you or not, you are ready for it! Just tell the world, Get ready, get ready, get ready!

> It is God himself who has made us what we are and given us new lives from Christ Jesus; and long ages ago he planned that we should spend these lives in helping others (Eph. 2:10, TLB).

My girls display different degrees of aggression, different qualities and different giftings. They are both absolutely

lovely and yet completely different. What I am trying to get you to see, daughters, is that beauty comes in all colors, shapes and sizes. It comes in different personalities and abilities. It is diverse and multiple. Never allow this world to stereotype you. You must not allow anyone to typecast you. They cannot determine what is acceptable for you. When He wanted you, He made you!

Now, girls, I write this word to you because I minister to many people who spend their lives in regret. They wish they were taller or smaller. They are always allowing other people to define beauty to them. They are in competition with other people. They are miserable. Many of them have great wealth and intellect. But, girls, the Bible says that godliness with contentment is great gain (1 Tim. 6:6). It means so much to be contented. You can't be contented until you develop an appreciation for yourself.

Avoid relationships with people who have no respect for themselves, because people never treat you better than they treat themselves. If they are self-abusers, they will be wife-abusers. They will abuse employees. They will abuse anyone or anything.

Contentment comes from within. It destroys jealousy and celebrates success in others. It doesn't matter what you accomplish, if you never master contentment you will die miserable. Whether you are famous or infamous, educated or illiterate, if you never learn contentment, you will never be free.

The great gain of the Bible is godliness, which is to continually be our goal, and contentment, which must become the nesting place where greatness is spawned. Your inner greatness will only be conceived when you lay back in the bed of contentment and appreciation for what God has put in you. Then your gift will bud and blossom, and we will all eat from the fruit of your wholeness!

We are all students now in the school of life. Heaven is

our only diploma. Any living person who isn't there hasn't graduated; they are still taking classes. You will learn from everyone. The discerning person learns wisdom from the idiot and folly from the intelligent. You must have the perception to look deeply into life and then apply what you see. You will see that every incident, every feeling, every fear is a class. Each one has its own curriculum. The ones who hurt you the worst teach you the best. Survival is taught in the wilderness. Loneliness is best taught in a crowd.

I encourage you to learn all that you can. At the same time, understand that you must learn from others without losing your core. Your essence may be cultivated, but do not allow anyone to mutilate who you were created to be. You are a survivor, and you can overcome anything; just always land on your feet. I don't want you to get lost in the maze of life and end up being something different from what you were designed to be. I know what you were designed to be. You came from good stock. We are not perfect. You will see many defects, but we are strong. We are children of the King!

Find people who enhance you rather than inhibit you. There are those among us who fertilize the gifted mind and give wind to the open sails. These are the associates you want to surround you. You must be surrounded by those persons who celebrate you. When you have been with people of quality, they will leave your sails full of air. Your feet will feel like running, and you will better see your own strengths through their eyes. Their insights will enhance you. You will grow from the pearls of wisdom that fall from their lips. You will also contribute your own precocious words of wisdom.

When you encounter those who try to tell you that you have little to offer, always remember to laugh. It is impolite to hear a joke and not laugh. Surely they jest. God never

made anyone that He didn't look back on and say it was good and very good. As a father I want to be the first man to tell you what the Father has already said: You are wonderful, full of potential. Possibility is written on your forehead. You can be anything you desire, but you can't be just anybody. Be yourself, because when you are who He made and what He made, He will always say, "It is good!"

> And God saw every thing that he had made, and, behold, it was very good. And the evening and the morning were the sixth day (Gen. 1:31, KJV).

You are born like a blank sheet of paper waiting to be written. You are the canvas on which time will create a collage of experience and faith. You are a melody that is waiting to be sung. You are prose whose lines are being formed and whose thoughts are yet being gathered. Be careful whose hand etches on your heart and writes in your life. You are off to a great start. Your possibilities are infinite and your potential endless. You are preprogrammed for success. I have prayed over you and watched you grow.

Nevertheless, I realize that you are not exempt from challenges and distress. So I write to prepare you for life's little unexpected events. Whether your challenge comes through failed marriage, morality or physical afflictions, you can still overcome. You are strong and creative, endowed and enabled. Never allow anyone or anything to deplete your confidence in your God. He is a loving Father, and He cares for you. His love is not contingent upon your performance. He has loved you without restriction.

> But God commendeth his love toward us, in that, while we were yet sinners, Christ died for us (Rom. 5:8, KJV).

This is what you must know. You must know the power of deletion. You must know that where pain leaves its scribbles, God erases the pain. If after all I have desired for you, poured in you and attempted to give you, there is still a broken place in you; if you find the wrong words are written in your life, once you have discovered them, do not give up and say, "This is all I can do or be."

Take advice from your natural father. I have often faced challenges, experienced pain and failed miserably. But life does have a delete button. Your heavenly Father is a God of second chances and new horizons. You are facing a rising sun. Always turn your back from the setting suns of life and wait through the night in the spirit of expectancy. There will always come a rising sun and a new day full of chances, new people and fresh possibilities. You see, the wonderful thing about being God's daughter is that He gives second chances by request.

Chapter Three

If You Should Ever Have a Need

*W*e have loved our children equally. There is absolutely no difference in the content of affection between how we love our boys and how we love our girls! I cannot express how strongly we care for the little ones who have been entrusted to us.

We have reared them differently. We express that love differently. My wife, being a woman and having never experienced life as a boy, is enamored by aspects of the boys' development that I am familiar with. I am familiar

with them because I already know exactly what it feels like to be a little boy or a young man. They are walking in footsteps my weary feet have already trod. I am wise to all of the intricate details of the discovery of maleness.

I prepare them for the next step because I am all too aware of what it takes to be a man. At the end of my preparations I pray, because I can prepare them for the challenges of their gender but not the challenges of their times. I do not know the world they will walk in. I can only prescribe the medicines that enabled me to survive my day. They will have to modify my prescriptions to the times in which they live.

They look to me for strength and example. They look to me for affirmation and guidance. But it is to their mother that they tend to come when they are in need. Her objective is less toward preparation. It is more toward gratification. She lives to see them happy; I live to see them ready!

When we walk down the hall into the bedroom of our little girls, their lace-clad, flower-strewn doll palace is the place where teaching seems of little consequence to me. It is here where I am enamored and overwhelmed by the mystique of their softness. Their fragile, silky voices need only suggest a need, and I will generally comply.

My wife, who loves them madly, is still more objective than I. She knows that she must prepare them for the unique strength that is required to be strong, resourceful women. She is preparing them for the blank checks of life. She must acquaint them with the challenges and the responsibilities that life demands, whether they are to be married or single, businesswomen or domestic queens.

Together we provide both training and impulsive affection. Through our unified efforts the children will at least experience the flavor of the uniqueness of our perspectives. God planned the family, and He has done a wonderful job.

Having said all of that, I must then begin to explain the

strong compulsion that comes over a father when he hears his daughter make a request. With a son's request, a father may comply. He may allow his son to wait if needed. The father knows that the wait will not hurt the son. OK, I admit it. It probably wouldn't hurt the girls either. But how is a guy to know that? He feels so protective. He wants to provide for her immediately. It is hard for me to express this without smiling.

I can hear my wife accusing me of spoiling the girls, an accusation that I fervently deny. If my daughters are in the car with me and merely whimper a faint entreaty for french fries or some other culinary delight, she says that I nearly wreck the car turning it around to go get what they want. I think she might be exaggerating slightly. But I will admit that I enjoy providing for all of my children.

Occasionally the soft feminine voices of my willowy little women may make me a little more accommodating than do the grunts of my boys, whose strong arms and backs do not suggest the degree of helplessness my ego needs to thrive. As the boys become older, they join me in helping to provide courage and strength to the girls in the house. Whatever the motive, I guess I am rather accommodating to the girls' requests. After all, they are so dainty; they need me!

I wonder how many women know what it feels like to be a father. It's a feeling that causes our chests to swell with pride when we lie down at night, sensing we have done a good job of providing for our families. Fearing for my family's safety, I have often walked through the house in the darkness of the night just to recheck a door or investigate a noise. My rest is broken if their safety is threatened.

I wonder how many women realize that they have a Father who never sleeps nor slumbers. He has assigned angels to compass about you and to ensure your safety. He will spare no expense to insure that you are safe. He will

not rest. He will arise with healing in His wings. He will come to you in a flash and stay with you through the night. He is the Everlasting Father. He doesn't leave, He doesn't desert, and He doesn't forsake you. He is there. What you must come to understand is that He cares so much for you. He wants you to have all that you need.

A thousand so-called feminists may erase *Father* out of the Bible and replace the word with a neutered term that they find less offensive. How can we be liberalists if being a liberalist runs the risk of eliminating distinctions? Has no one pointed out the difference between distinctions and discriminations? This is not the effort of well-meaning Bible scholars trying to find a contemporary word that doesn't alter the intended meaning of the text. This is a generation that says to God, "You are whatever we say You are."

It is so pathetic to think that changing a word in a book would change a gender in reality. If God represents Himself as a father, perhaps it is because He knows best what a father's love should represent. The offense is born in the heart of someone who has failed to understand that a father is a compliment to a woman and not an insult. Sadly, we have come to a time when the role of the father has been so mutilated that we have lost any real revelation into the breadth and depth of the Father's heart. How could any daughter be offended who has ever seen the broadening grin on the leathery face of a compassionate father whose greatest joy is seeing his daughter succeed?

A good father is not an insult to femininity. A good father is an avid fan of his daughter, a source of insulation from insult and adversity. He is there for her. He nurtures her.

Who has bewitched us that we have lost all sense of diversity? Have we become so sensitive that we pervert the plan of God and distort His Word for the sake of a political agenda? Hear me when I declare to you that the Father loves His girls. His heart cried through the prophet Jeremiah

for the healing of His daughters! He wants to see you blessed.

> For the brokenness of the daughter of my people I am broken; I mourn, dismay has taken hold of me. Is there no balm in Gilead? Is there no physician there? Why then has not the health of the daughter of my people been restored? (Jer. 8:21-22, NAS).

It is the Father's joy to provide for His daughters. Whatever the need, He longs to see it met. He cries through Jeremiah, "Is there no physician there?" In other words, Didn't I leave provision for their calamity? Their condition implied that He had failed to leave provisions. That was not true. He is Jehovah-jireh. He is the Father of provision. He is the reality of which Abraham was just a shadow. He is the giving God who loves to know that all of His children are blessed. He will bless His sons, who are created directly in His image and after His similitude. How much more would He have respect for the woman as the weaker vessel. Not weak in terms of substandard, but weak in terms of softer. A silk shirt is more delicate than a cotton one. But it is also more valuable. Weaker doesn't mean lesser — just softer, more satin-like!

> Likewise, ye husbands, dwell with them according to knowledge, giving honour unto the wife, as unto the weaker vessel, and as being heirs together of the grace of life; that your prayers be not hindered (1 Pet. 3:7, KJV).

Here the Father is teaching men to give honor unto the wife as unto the weaker vessel. The term *honor* explains that the term *weaker* is not a comparison of quality but an expression of sensitivity. It is an honor to be treated as more fragile, with love and caring. The *New Strong's*

Exhaustive Concordance of the Bible defines *time,* the Greek word for *honor,* in the following manner:

> *time* (tee-may'); a value, i.e. money paid, or (concretely and collectively) valuables; by analogy, esteem (especially of the highest degree), or the dignity itself: KJV — honour, precious, price, [sum].

God doesn't tell men to honor women because He loves them more than men. Rather, God is expressing the need to handle His daughters differently from His sons. Daughter material is more fragile, though that doesn't mean of lesser quality. Can you see that His level of love is the same, but His mode of expression is different?

We need distinction. Distinction can exist without discrimination. Enjoy who you are. One of the greatest tragedies occurs when women fight their way to the place of being treated like men. The tragedy becomes apparent as they later realize that the real honor would have been to be recognized and honored as women.

I know, dear daughters, that there will be those who try to demean and belittle you. They will try to discriminate against you because you are women. Fight not for equality but for neutrality. Your distinctions are too valuable to forfeit. There are some benefits that go along with being who you are and being whose you are. Your Father is the King, and you are His daughters, His princesses. You need only ask Him, and He has the power to move in your behalf.

If you would come to Him as your Father and understand that you are His princesses, His daughters, His joy, what a miracle would happen as you lose your inhibitions in the strength of His loving. These are the arms that threaten enemies and chase away assailants. But they are also the tender, caring arms of the affectionate Father who is vulnerable to the cry of His seed! Your prayer life will literally explode when you realize that the Father longs to bless you.

My daughters, when you were small and you would run toward me with saggy diapers, as a natural father I was there. Although sometimes the odors were pungent, and the accident those diapers hid was strong enough to make me want to put you down, still love would pick you up.

This is the love that God has for you, only a thousand times more real. There will be times you will be afraid to run to Him, knowing that He can easily tell that you have had an accident. Never be afraid of Him. As weak as I am, I loved you enough to hold you till I could wash you. How much greater is His love than mine! This is the love that comes from the Father who knows that the smell of the mistake will pass, but the love for the daughter will last! Don't be afraid of your Father. He already knows you have made and will make mistakes. He will pick you up if you ask Him.

I am telling you this in case you ever have a need. If you ever need someone who will be there no matter how complicated the problem, He will be there. The stench of your failure will never overwhelm the fragrance of His love. He adores you. How would you know this unless some man tells you the intensity of a father's love? I am afraid you will have needs and try foolishly to meet them on your own. As one hymn writer so wisely stated:

> Oh what peace we often forfeit,
> Oh what needless pain we bear,
> All because we do not carry
> Everything to God in prayer.

Many times we fail to go to the Father who can help, and instead we run straight into the arms of someone who cannot help. Oh, sure, I'd love to see you married and rearing children if that is what you want as well. But understand that you must not marry someone thinking he can save you. Men are not saviors. They have nothing with which to save you. We men are heirs, together with our

wives, of the grace of life. We are both eligible for inheritance. We do not give the inheritance. We need it just like
our wives do.

So, dear daughters, don't be fooled into looking to the
arms of flesh for healings that come from the arms of God.
If you choose to marry, don't marry out of what you need.
Marry out of the abundance of what you have to offer.
When two people enter into a relationship for what they
can receive, they are both disappointed. I love you too
much to see you disappointed.

No man, no matter how wonderful, can wipe all tears
from your eyes. Your life will bring many tears. They are
unavoidable. They are a part of existence. Pleasure and
pain, sunshine and rain are all intermingled with day-to-day
survival. There are going to be scrapes and scratches,
bruises and brokenness, that neither your husband nor your
natural father can heal. I want you to know where to go
when life is too much.

Now I hope I will always be there to answer your questions and hold your hand. I hope I will be there when
you graduate and achieve various levels of success. I want
to be the one who walks down the aisle with you when
you have found whoever it is that lights the flame within
your eyes.

Greater still, I want to be there when your world seems
cold and your friends seem few. I hope I'll be there to usher
you through the dark places I have often faced myself. I
would die shielding you, praying for you or just loving you.
But I might be gone before the gray clouds come and the
rain falls. I would hate to say good-bye before you have
kissed your star and found your rainbow. But I am not afraid
as long as I have a chance to tell you about your other
Father. He is stronger than I and much better than I. He has
helped me to give you all that I have. It was His hand behind
mine. It was His arm within mine. Every blessing you have

ever received *through* me came *from* Him. You will never be alone. He has spoiled me so that I can spoil you.

If He chooses to love you directly, then I can but step aside. I have been a middle man for Him. I know I haven't done it as well as He would, but I have really been blessed describing His love through my mouth and His kisses through my lips. I have just enjoyed letting Him love you through me. I want to be His conduit of expression and His release of compassion. I enjoyed hearing His voice sing through me. He has helped me immeasurably. He fed you. It was with my hand, but He fed you all the while. Your mother may not know it, but the best moments of our lives were the moments when He was shining through me. He has really made me look good! But, alas, I must reveal my sources and unveil my strength just in case a problem arises and you find you have a need.

There may be a day when life takes a turn, and I won't be able to speak a word. At the very least I can tell you about your other Father now. He will surely outlive me. He is wiser than I, and He can do anything. I know it is hard for you to believe or for me to imagine, but He loves you even more than I do. I am just glad that I know Him. Some fathers didn't know Him, and that is why they never told their daughters about Him. Some may never have meant to fail their daughters, but they never knew the pattern and they had no one to copy! Nevertheless, there are no excuses. Every father should tell his daughter about her other Father in case she ever has a need.

There will always be needs. We all have them, both men and women. We have so many needs that we can never assure each other that we can fulfill each other. Real fulfillment comes from God. He is the only One who can encompass every need and fulfill every desire. I want you to have a relationship. It is honorable to be married if that is your choice. Just understand that whoever God sends into

your life will be limited and human. They will give a measure of comfort, but real wholeness comes from God alone. There are some areas in your life that God has reserved for Him alone. He will heal them and fill them. No one else can.

I recommend Him because He has been my trusted friend and confidant. He has never betrayed me or divulged a secret. He is the strong, silent type. He knows when to keep still. When nights are cold and days are dreary, He is a comfort and a peace. He is to the soul what hot tea is to the body. He strengthens and warms the chill of life for those who will trust Him. He is the provision for the problem and the solution to the challenges that life will surely present.

You need not impress Him. He already knows who you are. He has searched you and known you (Ps. 139:1). There is no need to try to project an image. He has seen you in the raw. He has examined your thoughts and known your imaginations. You feel somewhat vulnerable, realizing that whatever you are trying to discuss with Him, He already knows. But the healing balm flows into the bleeding places of life when you realize that this omniscient knowledge of you has not caused Him to forsake you. He is still there.

What a love! Love at its apex is when you have seen the worst in a person and yet have not forsaken him. This is the love that your heavenly Father has for you. Why do I want you to know this? Because I don't want you to be one of the foolish women who run from the only answer there is to the questions of life. You need never run from Him. You need never run from me. He made up His mind about you before the worlds were framed, and so have I.

This is not the standard of love that you are to seek from men. It is not the instrument with which men are to be measured. You will never find a man like Him. This love that I speak about is the love that God gives to compensate

the thirsting heart that has drunk from the waters of men's promises, and still the need is unabated. It is the brook that we come to when no other has quenched the thirstiness of life. It is the cool refreshing knowledge of a love that calms the desperate cravings and clingings that others will develop. They will grope and fight to have the touch of men whose arms can ease no pain. But you won't. For I have told you of the only One whose kiss can curse pain and ease fears, just in case you have a need.

I love you too much to allow you to join the masses of women who are chasing wildly after the affections of some fictional lover whose shiny armor is a mere fantasy that will never be humanly realized. I cannot allow you to become bitter as you rummage through relationships looking for divine love from human hearts. I will not allow you to think that there is somewhere beneath the sun's bright light a hero who isn't tarnished with human flaws. If you are to love a man, understand that he is a man. You will never be disappointed by what you don't expect.

In short, my daughters, my sweetness, whatever you need, whether natural or spiritual, God is the source from which your blessings must come. You will not look to men. It may come through men, but not from them. All of your help will come from the Lord. He will use people from time to time. But your deepest needs He will fill Himself. He alone can give the soul release. Man sets bones, but God causes them to knit together. Man gives love, but God fills voids. Whatever the arena, remember to include Him.

Redeem your treasures through His Word. If they are not from His Word, they are not from Him. You want only the answer that comes from Him. Patience is going to be the real challenge. It is difficult to learn to wait. When you feel that you need something today and God doesn't answer readily, you must learn to trust Him and wait. Anything you provide yourself will only increase the struggle. Wait on His

blessings and His timing, and you will have the kind of blessings that add no sorrow.

> The blessing of the Lord, it maketh rich, and he addeth no sorrow with it (Prov. 10:22, KJV).

That is what a good father wants for his daughter — blessings without sorrow. I know that I cannot shield you from all pain. I know that pain is an instrument of correction and a conduit for power. Nevertheless, I shudder to think of you bearing more than your share. I want the pains of life to be held to a minimum by godly counsel. So I speak to you from my heart, and I counsel you with my pen. Look to God when there are needs in your life. He satisfies. Like calm sheep grazing tranquilly in the afternoon sun, you will find fulfillment for your soul and contentment with yourself.

Nervous wanderings, frantic cravings and desperate clingings will dissipate in the light of His smile and the understanding that you are not alone.

Now there are countless women in our world who have been abused. Many have been molested and some ostracized. They come in all colors, ages and sizes. Many wrap their secrets in furs and dress them up with jewelry. Some are staggering down city streets in tattered clothing. In a guttural voice they shout obscenities and vulgarities. Both kinds are bitter and in pain. They have never known love and tenderness. Their lives have been a series of disappointments and distresses. When you find them, tell them that there is a Father who does not abuse or rape, rob or demean. Tell them that He is the One who enabled them to survive the dark places. Tell them He is real.

He is the One who enables the broken to break without falling apart. He is the One who holds the feeble and comforts the broken. He is the Father who rocks the street woman to sleep and holds the beaten prostitute through the

night. He is the One who stopped the gun from going off. He is the One who eased the addict's pain and gave rest to the nervous and strength to the trembling. He is the Father of the fatherless. They may not know that He got them home many nights when others would have devoured them. He has parented them through circumstances and fed them through the hand of strangers. He hasn't forgotten the less fortunate or the more fearful. He puts His loving oint-ments on the secrets of our lives.

Tell them, my daughters, that He is faithful. They should not blame Him for their pain. They should thank Him for their survival. He is the night watchman who saves the wounded hearts of broken daughters and gives them the gift of tomorrow.

My two dear daughters, you are not orphans. You have not been forsaken by your father or rejected by your mother. We are here; even if we were not, you would still not be orphaned because you have another Father who will always watch out for you. When you awake in a fright and feel your room closing in on you, understand that He is there. When those with whom you work have chided you and embarrassed you and life seems unfair, He is still there. Whenever tragedy arises and unmade decisions rage in your mind, remember I taught you to trust in a God who will not fail. I taught you what I believe. I taught you what has brought me through the storm. I taught you in case you awake and find me sleeping. I taught you in case you have a need.

> But my God shall supply all your need according
> to his riches in glory by Christ Jesus. Now unto
> God and our Father be glory for ever and ever.
> Amen (Phil. 4:19-20, KJV).

There is a difference between wants and needs. There are many things that you will want and some that you will

intensely desire. That doesn't necessarily mean you will have them. There will be many desires that are born in your heart through other sources. Some will come from your peers and friends. Some will come from your age and stage in life. There will be times when things as inanimate as a television set will influence what you feel you need. Amidst all of these influences, God will not grant to you everything you suggest. A good father doesn't give in to every whim. He decides carefully what is best for his daughters.

It is going to require faith, but you must with maturity begin to conclude that if God doesn't grant it, you don't need it. You may want it; but if it were a need, He would have supplied it. He promised to do it. You don't have to beg or plead. You don't have to manipulate or pout. If God has promised, His Word is sure. That means that when there is a discrepancy between what you think you need and what is being supplied, remember God cannot lie. If it were for your good — if it were a need, emotionally, physically or spiritually — He would supply it.

Now caution, my dear daughters. Remember that you are to prosper and be in good health as your soul prospers (3 John 2). If your soul is not prospering, that is the primary need. Nothing should be of greater concern than that. Every other supply is going to flow "as your soul prospers" (NAS). That is why you must be sure that you maintain a healthy heart for God and a sound mind. For what would it profit you as a woman to gain this whole world and lose your soul (Mark 8:36)?

Don't lose your soul (mind, memory and affections) over things. Don't stress out or burn out, become jealous or enter into warfare over things. They will not profit if your values are misconstrued. Keep your head in the right place. Seek the kingdom and His righteousness, and all these things, whatever they are, shall be added unto you (Matt. 6:33). Why? Because they will come to you as your soul prospers.

If you are reading this book and your whole life has been ransacked, the very first thing you should do is make sure you are in a right relationship with Jesus Christ. It does matter. When you are in right standing with Him, you have a guarantee that if something is a need He will supply it. It may not come when you think you should have it, but it will come when you need it most.

Are things right between you and your heavenly Father? Are you on speaking terms with Him? Are you submitting your life to His Word? Submitting means more than attending church. Is your sexuality under His control? How many areas of your life can He come into? These are the kinds of questions that need an answer in case you ever have a need.

I am wondering if you would pray with me. I am wondering as you face the hard challenges of making changes to be the daughter that He wants you to be, would you allow me to pray with you? I know so well how hard it is to deal with one's own self. There are these bondages that overwhelm us. There are relationships that ensnare us. We need divine help. Would you pray this simple prayer?

> Dear Lord,
> I come in Jesus' name. I am tired of doing things my own way. I realize I have not been honest before You, and I have not been the kind of daughter that You would be pleased with. Thank You for loving me in spite of myself. You have been good to me. I repent for the shame I may have caused You. I want to be in right standing with You. Give me victory over myself. I say yes to You as You become Lord in my life. I give You even those areas I have been holding back for myself. I want You to begin to restore what sin has destroyed in my life. Thank You, Father, for helping me over the hurdles of life. Amen.

Chapter ❤ *Four*

Fatherless Girls, Fearful Women and Faithfulness

$\mathcal{N}$ow you and I both know that there is no such thing as a fatherless girl. Not really. Every girl has a biological father, or at least a man who contributed his seed toward her production.

The tragedy, however, is the reality that donating sperm to an open womb doesn't make a father. Neither does birthing a child make a mother. The real truth of the matter is that a father's role is greatest after birth, not before. It is not the conception of the child that presents the challenge of fatherhood. It is the rearing of the child that determines whether a man is just a donor or a father in the true sense.

Many men do not realize how important it is that there be a father figure somewhere in the house. Even many women do not realize that it is helpful and healthy to have a loving, responsible father in the home with his children. Each of us, the mother and the father, contributes different things to the totality of development. When the father is not there, there is a loss and a void that affects all aspects of the children's lives and even the mother from which they were born. Fathers are not optional like extra equipment in a car. They are needed, and when they are not present there is pain.

It is obvious that a father is significant to the well-being of a young man. It is from our fathers that we receive the first pattern we can expect to resemble in some way. It helps to be able to contour our rough edges in alignment with someone we admire. I can still remember my fascination with the hair on my father's chest and checking periodically to see if there were any traces of peach fuzz collecting on my rather bald chest. I figured he represented what I would be someday. It is easy, therefore, to understand that the absence of a father leaves a male child without the desired mentoring and object of emulation.

Unfortunately, the subject of a father's effect on daughters is a far less explored subject. I do not want to imply that healthy, normal children cannot be reared in fragmented homes or by single parents. I am just pointing out that in God's divine plan both parents were there to assist in the nurturing process. A daughter watches her father and draws conclusions as to what men are like. She watches and studies her father to ascertain what a male does and does not accept well. It is on this safe perch of childhood that she can take notes that will assist her in later years. She can determine that men are stable or unstable, reckless or

responsible. This is why we as fathers have such an awesome responsibility. We are, with our actions, defining the
next generation's point of reference. Her husband will be
weighed on the scales of what her father was or was not to
her and her mother.

Furthermore, many men fail to realize that some women
are traumatized by childhood problems that range in com-
plexity from the type of fathers that were silent and aloof
to the far more tragic cases of molestation or physical
abuse. Some were reared in homes where their mothers
were poorly treated. Some were reared in homes where
their fathers were passive and their mothers dominated. All
of these circumstances affect her imagery and perception of
maleness. For many women from these backgrounds, it is a
challenging task to dismiss the imagery that haunts the
recesses of their minds and to enter into a relationship.

My dear daughters, I hope that there are enough positive examples in this world to give you some sort of idea
of the kind of man who is worth your attention and affection. It is my hope that my treatment of you as a father
would set some precedent for the standard you require
from other men who will later enter into a place of signifi-
cance in your lives. I can certainly confirm that there are
many lovely ladies whose definition of manhood did not
start as pleasantly as yours. For them it is a real struggle to
regain their balance in heterosexual relationships.

You see, when there is no father in the home, it can
affect the daughter in many ways. Some are so starved for
male approval that what should be a normal attraction to
men is accelerated into an obsessive need for male affirmation. Tragically, these dear ladies allow themselves to be
devoured in the arms of men who have neither regard nor
respect for them as people. Dear girls, understand that there
is a vast difference between sex and love. There will be
voids in your life. Regardless of my presence in your life,

there will still be voids. There will be places of lack and areas that I failed to affirm or you failed to receive. Just understand that gluttony does not heal starvation. It is just another type of disorder. If you have been starved in some area, realize that becoming a glutton does not heal the lack of early years.

Most people enter into relationships for gratification. Sexual gratification is just the tip of the iceberg. We really are trying to find the arms that we missed in childhood. We want to feel desired and affirmed, comforted and safe. Just understand that when there is a lack in your life, it takes God to heal it. Otherwise you will find yourself reaching out to men for a restoration that only God can give. If all of us are vulnerable in these areas that remain unresolved, can you imagine how tough it must be for the girl who has never felt loved by her father?

Some women secretly carry guilt that they have misappropriated as daughters, thinking it was their fault that their fathers didn't stay with their mothers. They are always trying to prove something to themselves. I will tell you now that growing up is hard work. It is even tougher when today's woman is wrestling with yesterday's little girl. Somewhere deep beneath the painted smiles and polished nails is a longing, an aching, a void. Somewhere beneath the symbols of success lurks a feeling of incompleteness.

The emptiness taints their successes and taunts their accomplishments. They are either distrustful of men as a whole or they idealize a man's attention as the epitome of success and fulfillment. They are afraid to be alone. They feel as if they have been alone all of their lives, and they fight the feeling by adding people to their lives. If they were wise they would know that having people in your life, in your house or even in your bed doesn't insure that you will not be lonely. But if they really come to know God, they could be alone and still not be lonely. It is when they

achieve the gift of being alone that they are really ready to share their companionship with someone else.

Daughters, I believe that whenever someone is involved with you, they become a part of what was going on in you before they came around. For some men that is traumatic because if the woman isn't happy before he comes, she will soon be unhappy with him around. She will go from madly in love to distant and frustrated because she expected him to be all that she didn't get out of life. At first she is excited. Later she is disappointed because she realizes that she is still involved with a wound from her past. It is a void that only the Holy Spirit can fill.

Most Christians are seated so high on their perch of self-righteousness that they often fail to minister to the pain behind the sin. They are concerned about the habits of sin. But they don't seem to understand that removing the act doesn't free the heart. It just represses a problem that manifests in cynicism and frustration. People are teachable when they are not in pain. It is like telling a child not to scratch a rash. She will do it even if she does it in her sleep because she is feeling the discomfort. But if you can apply the ointment that eases the discomfort, the habit is easily broken.

I am sorry we live in a world filled with pain and rashes. I am sorry we live in a world filled with imperfections and scars. But, in all of my searching, the only thing I have found to offer you that will soothe the itching for affection and the bleeding from scars is Jesus.

Many women you encounter will be inflamed with the frustrations and the discontentment that come from their need to be affirmed by a masculine image. Some will have reached a point where they have become embittered by the lack of positive male examples. They will throw themselves into careers, education or some other demand to avoid the battle of the sexes. God never intended for it to be a battle. He intended one to complement the other. But when complementing is deferred long enough, there will be an irritation. I call it a rash. It is an itch that is difficult to scratch. Thank God for Jesus. He medicates the things that frustrate, eventually eliminating the entire struggle in the hearts of those who trust in Him.

His presence is the medicine that women and men alike need to avoid obsessions and extremes that accompany disorders and dysfunctions. He is literally the balm that, if applied regularly and completely, can break the habits that we all wrestle to control! He is balm for every woman and every man whose life has been injured by something they received. He provides even for those whose pain stems from the starving reminders of what they didn't receive. He is the bread of heaven, and if they take Him in He will satisfy.

My daughters, when you were growing up in the same house with me, you learned the effects of feminine charm. You learned how to move me, and you learned how to make me smile. You learned boundaries — what Daddy will tolerate, what Mommy will tolerate and so on. Soon you knew which one of us to ask for what. You were filled with psychological discernment, naturally endowed and bountifully applied. You analyzed everything in the house. You are bright. These insights will help you with your relationships later, because it is here that you began to prepare for tomorrow.

You could move me with a smile. You could melt my most stern resolve with a kiss. Your bragging about me made me perform in your behalf. These basic realities are true with all men. That type of kindness is not challenging or threatening; any man responds well to positive reinforcement. Even God responds to praise! It is not manipulative to know this. It is manipulative when you only praise to gain influence rather than birthing that praise from a sincere heart that appreciates the warm love of a giving God.

Even when the answer is no you must know how far is too far. As a little girl you knew when it was not a good time to bring up an issue. You learned instinctively when I was irritable. Somehow your watchful eye soon would catch a wrinkle on my brow, and you would even be able to tell your mother, "Daddy is tired. We will talk later. This is Daddy time." It helps you to understand the complexities of our gender. It helps you to become familiar with problem-solving with the opposite sex. It further helps you not to be insulted by a difference of opinion.

Women who didn't learn to recognize that Daddy time when they were growing up are far more apt to see a disagreement as a terminal, insurmountable dilemma because they are not familiar with the difference in the thought patterns of men and women. The answer no to your question doesn't mean that you are rejected, just that your idea is.

This is invaluable in preparing you for later life. It is important that you have a point of reference for fatherhood. It takes the mystique away from masculinity. We are often intimidated by what we don't understand. That kind of intimidation can lead to the demise of an entire relationship. It is the lack of negotiation skills that destroys the potential for long-range relationships. Even in your prayer life you can better relate to your heavenly Father as you realize that a no to your request doesn't challenge His commitment to you or His affection for you.

When we understand something we are not afraid of it. Some women come from abusive backgrounds. They either were victimized or were witnesses to abusive situations. If not ministered to, these women can be left with a leery feeling where men are concerned. Even though many have not lost their attraction to the male, they still have a basic distrust of the one to whom they are attracted. They are sometimes left wrestling with fear or suppressed rage. They appear jealous, but they are not jealous as much as they are tormented by fear. They can appear argumentative and disgruntled. They are afraid of rejection and pain. They are afraid of losing and disappointment. They are afraid of history repeating itself.

My mother used to say that a burnt child dreads fire. Her illustration is applicable because we dread things from the past that we associate with discomfort and pain. It keeps us from being whole and confident. When you consider a need to be healed or loosed from trauma, it would be a God-given gift to live as if what happened had not happened. God gives us grace not only to overcome the things we face but also to overcome the effects of the things we face.

The enemy doesn't want these women to be able to run to their heavenly Father and be healed, because they will then live as if the trauma had never occurred. Therefore, even when it comes to approaching God, the enemy makes them a little uncomfortable when they kneel down and say, "Our Father." That term, *Father*, doesn't give them the comfort that it does to others. They are tormented by a memory. They are wrestling with a distrust that aborts their faith and destroys their confidence.

"Our Father," they say. What is that? To them a father may be someone who left and did not return. To some a father is someone whose hands lingered too long on the soft skin of their inner thighs — a father who lied to their mother and betrayed their family trust. To them a father may be someone whose belt and angry words filled the house with terror. When they hear the word *father*, they smell liquor. They hear heavy breathing and slurred speech. They hear grunting and recall gropings and secrets. They remember secret smiles and lewd looks stolen at dinner tables while mother was looking in another direction. They feel no closeness, and they have no trust. They are just afraid.

They associate the problem with the gender rather than

with the person who inflicted the pain. They feel as though all men are the same. This is a prejudice that we have never marched about. There is no legislation against this prejudice. Yet homes all over America are being destroyed by prejudiced concepts where abused and mistreated persons have survived an injury but are scarred with a stereotyped definition of what men are all about. Many a good husband has lost the wife he loved to memories that have tormented her all of her life. She couldn't quite seem to trust him or anyone else who looked like the one who hurt her. She is a woman whom God wants to loose! He wants to loose her so that she can be free to love herself, her husband, her life and even her God.

Her fear of a father may be stopping her from believing God's Word for her blessing, her healing or her miracle. She needs to know that God can be trusted. She will say she trusts Him, but under pressure she keeps taking back the thing she just turned over to Him. She will have a tendency to be domineering or even overbearing. Many misunderstand her dominance and think that she is arrogant or hard to please. However, in many cases she is just afraid of counting on anyone other than herself.

She will tell you, "If I don't do it, it doesn't get done." She is self-reliant and self-sufficient, but worse still, self-consumed. Self-reliance is not a bad trait unless it alienates other people God has sent into your life to be a blessing. If she is not careful, she will even infect her daughter with that miserable aloneness and same spirit of distrust. She doesn't realize that she is passing her dysfunction on to the next generation. She is filled with bitterness and finds it difficult to release the pain.

What can she do? She has cried; she has prayed. She lies on the floor like a bird whose broken wing has stopped the flight that should have been. She sings her song from the ground. Her helpless flapping comes out as temper tantrums, mood swings, addictive behavior or compulsive affairs. She is miserable. She is trapped. She ages, grays and becomes weaker without becoming wiser. Trapped in a time warp, she relives little girl issues in a woman's body. She is trapped between ages and stages of life — too much of a woman to be a little girl, but too much of a little girl to be a woman. The child in her has imprisoned the woman in her. When no one is around, the little girl in her sheds tears, silent tears that sneak down painted cheeks, tears whose descent goes unnoticed because all would-be comforters have been chased away.

What can she do? you ask. How can she break free? Well, the first thing she needs to do is isolate the problem from the gender. She needs to understand that all men are not the same. Isolating the problem brings healing. When she isolates her problem she puts it in quarantine and forbids it to infect all areas of her life. When she isolates it she stops the enemy from using it to rob her of good moments in the present because of bad moments in the past. Like a cancer it must be isolated and removed!

Second, she must allow God's love to pierce through the pain. It must be God's love first, not man's, because God's love is the only love that is perfect enough to pass her stringent test. His love is perfect and will cast out fear (1 John 4:18). His love will restore to her the opportunity for the little girl in her to have a loving relationship with a Father who will not fail. Love is God's gift given against pain. She can come right now and lay her head upon His strong breast and be healed. There is no molestation in God; He will not abuse her. She can trust Him. It is with Him that she learns to unleash the love she has locked up within.

But it must not stop with God. When she is whole she will be able to love others, even others who are imperfect and have flaws, without having flashbacks and associating today with yesterday. Out of the wholeness of her relationship

with Jesus she can regain the courage to experience love and life with others. It is a born-again experience. It is a freedom. It is God raising or nurturing a woman who is wrestling with little girl issues. It is a chance to do it over again and this time get it right.

Out of the wellsprings of her relationship with her heavenly Father she may be able to mend the breaches and repair the damages that have caused a degree of dysfunction to develop in her natural relationships. The wholeness that is reconstructed through her relationship with the Father helps her to understand, appreciate and develop a comfort zone with men. Beyond having a point of reference that dispels the mystique of the masculine personality, she also has a comfort zone in prayer that is less suspicious and more faith-filled.

One of the greatest things that all of us are afforded as Christians is the opportunity to receive restoration in our areas of depletion. Thank God that we have a Lord who can be touched by the feeling of our infirmities (Heb. 4:15)! He is able to minister to the voids in us. This ministry brings us to wholeness. That wholeness in turn makes it possible to live as if the brokenness had never occurred. We are like the vessel that is marred in the hand of the potter. He is a master at reshaping damage that has occurred through the course of living.

I challenge you as you develop as a woman to resist the temptation to live in a vacuum. When you encounter women whose broken pasts have left them suspicious of the male gender as a whole, remind them that wholeness enables us to love the imperfect. We must be careful that we don't preach false hope — the idea that there are perfect men who can be trusted not to disappoint. That is neither true nor realistic. Nor is it true that those women who demand such can themselves live up to those standards. It is a trick the enemy uses to stop you from enjoying life. It is a lofty expectation that is fictitious and nonexistent. People do fail. Men fail. Women fail. Children fail. But thanks be to God, He does not fail!

His unfailing love, when graciously bestowed upon us, enables us to love the imperfect. When He loves us we realize He does it in spite of what He knows about us. What a healing! What a lesson He teaches us when He loves us in spite of our failures and misalignments. The real challenge is to receive His love and learn to become secure enough to emulate that love in our relationships. Without that, we will have tremendous standards but absolutely no companionship. The walls that we build to protect us actually imprison us, and time escapes like sand trickling through an hourglass.

My dear daughters, remember God enables you to experience a level of faith that makes you a joy to be with. He heals you until you have no need to live in a vacuum. He brings you to the point where you can be free even from broken beginnings. So tell every woman you meet that even if her beginnings were less than what she hoped, God heals. Tell her that even if she had no father image or the father image she grew up with was distorted or perverted, Christ makes it possible to redefine what it means to have a father. He can assist her in her search to understand the masculine heart.

Some of the ladies you encounter will have spent all their lives in promiscuity. They have always suffered from low self-esteem. They are so starved for male attention that they will accept it by the hour, the night or the weekend. They need to know a real relationship with God will heal the void. Then when they are ready to enter into a relationship with a man, it will be for the right reason and not that insatiable thirsting for attention and affirmation that causes the relationships to be destroyed.

I write to you as a father who is imperfect and fragmented but nevertheless in love with three generations of femininity.

My daughters, from your grandmother, to your mother, to you, I love you. Each age and each relationship is a different spectrum of a beautiful collage of color and life.

Men are only human, and they are marred with flaws. I have tried to give you everything. I will fail. I am made of clay. Wherever I miss it, hold it against no other. But turn to the God who makes up the differences in life and balances the books for those who believe in His name. It is He who gives grace to the humble (James 4:6). He is the word of encouragement that is given to all those girls whose fathers forsook them and who suffered mistreatment in life. He is the leverage that gives stability to what would otherwise be an unfair circumstance. He is the Father they never had — the perfecter of the fathers whose love or wisdom failed.

When you meet those women around you whose emptiness perverts their fulfillment and tarnishes their successes, just tell them about the perfection of God's love. When they know His love then maybe His girls can love themselves also. To be able to love is a wonderful gift. Without it life is reduced to an existence filled with bland days and an empty collection of dusty trophies, with no eyes to view them and no hands to wipe them. Being alone is not the tragedy. It is being empty and bitter, suspicious and cynical. The tragedy is when God has provided someone to love these women, and they unknowingly and unwisely bark them away. Their bitterness becomes their only companion. I don't want that for you. I am writing all the wisdom I have collected through all that God has shown and all that I have concluded. Collectively, we in concert declare, Resist it at all cost!

It is my prayer that you be balanced. To be balanced is to be whole. To be balanced is to resist the temptation to be obsessed or extreme. To be balanced is to resist the temptation to be drunk or influenced by any intoxicant, whether that intoxicant comes as a drug or a disappointment.

Sobriety is a gift from God. It strengthens your discernment and makes you better able to steady your course and stay your hand.

You are strong, you are gifted and you are blessed — blessed from your mother's womb. You are a gift born out of the will and the mandates of God. You are uniquely endowed with gifts and talents that will never be duplicated and cannot successfully be imitated. You are awesome. Breathe in life and seize it in your hand. Turn your course, steady your mind and reach for the stars — all things are possible to the one who can believe. You are not limited by your past. You are only limited by the weights you refuse to release. Let them go and stretch out your hand to catch the stars.

> Wherefore seeing we also are compassed about with so great a cloud of witnesses, let us lay aside every weight, and the sin which doth so easily beset us, and let us run with patience the race that is set before us (Heb. 12:1, KJV).

That's what you must do: Lay aside every hindrance and run, girls. Go for it. Hold your head up, fill your lungs with air, stretch your legs and go for it. I want to assure you that the prize is always before you and never behind you. Many people think their best days are over, but that is not true. They are stunted by paralysis of vision and stagnancy of expectation. Regardless of past accomplishments, joys or wonderful moments, there are still fresh opportunities. Life has many prizes that you may receive if you stretch your legs and steady your vision. Remember to keep the past behind you and the future in front of you. I want to assure you that you cannot run forward if you keep looking back.

Chapter Five

The Right to Choose

*T*have always wanted you to know that you were valuable. One of the ways I tried to enforce that was by respecting you while I was rearing you. Neither your mother nor I made a practice of saying painful things that undermined your self-esteem. I believe you can correct a child without maiming their self-image. I don't have to attack who you are to reprimand what you did. I want you to be accustomed to good treatment.

I particularly want you to associate men with good

treatment. Therefore, when you encounter one who doesn't treat you well, it will be so unfamiliar that you will find it repulsive. If abuse is not checked, it reproduces itself in future relationships. I know from years of pastoring that most abuse victims wrestle with low self-esteem. They unfortunately choose to surround themselves with familiar personality types. These types, though often cruel and insulting, feel familiar to them.

It always seems odd to me that some victims in later years actually avoid good treatment. They seem leery of people who admire them and are more comfortable with people who criticize them. It is not because they enjoy being criticized. It is simply that criticism is familiar, and they find the insults believable. They might think, How could someone really love me like he says he does? I don't trust him! So the person who doesn't build them up but constantly points out their deficiencies seems more realistic to them.

Bottom line: I want you to be careful what you get used to. If you don't watch out, you can become accustomed to negative things, things the Father never wanted you to have, like pain or abuse. Some people have become used to poverty. Some have become used to fighting. They feel at home in pain. They cleave to it because they understand it.

My daughters, if inadvertently you have managed to pick up any of these characteristics, renounce them right now in the name of Jesus. You can change your mind. When I was a child, I was taught that it is a woman's prerogative to change her mind. If you have become accustomed to something you should get rid of, I want you to stop what you are doing and change your mind. I know it isn't easy, but it is so necessary. It will help you immeasurably to speak to yourself and say, I am better than this! You don't have to change the other person's mind. You just need to change your own.

And be not conformed to this world: but be ye transformed by the renewing of your mind, that ye may prove what is that good, and acceptable, and perfect, will of God (Rom. 12:2, KJV).

Some women have made it their life's goal to win someone whom they may never win. Or they have spent years trying to change the mind of someone who may not ever change. They will get angry and give the man the ultimatum. They will say to him, "Make up your mind whether you want her or me!" They are asking him to decide something they should be deciding. The real victory occurs when you change your own mind. The power of choice is a great power. Be careful that you do not give that power away. It is your right to choose how you want to live. Even God respects that right. He gives you the right to choose.

I call heaven and earth to record this day against you, that I have set before you life and death, blessing and cursing: therefore choose life, that both thou and thy seed may live (Deut. 30:19, KJV).

Instead of asking the abuser if he has had enough, you must ask yourself if you have had enough. This is always the greater question. Others may not ever get their fill of abusing you. If you have judged within yourself that abuse is not God's will for you, why are you asking someone else to choose? The greater question is, Do you, as a daughter of the King, want to live in this circumstance? God can change the other person's heart, and many women have survived to see that wonderful miracle happen. There are others whose lives have been consumed in a fit of rage by someone who refused to get well. These are life's challenges and choices. The decision is always yours. Make it wisely if you are ever confronted with it. A parent cannot make these choices for you. Yet, hopefully, prayer has burnt enough character in

you to trust the Christ that lives in you to empower you as you grow. Just remember, never ask someone else to answer your question.

God is too wise to let your deliverance be predicated on someone else's opinion. He will speak to you. When healing the sick, Jesus said, "According to your faith be it unto you" (Matt. 9:29, KJV). He is saying that basically it is up to you. Dear daughters, do you remember *The Wizard of Oz?* Dorothy was running up the yellow brick road looking for someone to help her get home. She faced disappointment when she realized that the wizard of Oz wasn't who she thought he was, and she was still lost.

To me the greatest line of that story was when little Dorothy finally realized that all she had to do was click her heels and she could go home anytime she wanted. If you remember, she was shocked because she kept thinking she needed someone else to help her get home. She finally realized that she could have gone home whenever she got ready. She had the power all the time! That is what I am saying to you. By God's rich grace you have the power. Don't forfeit it or forsake it. You can change your situation whenever you get ready.

Don't you see that you don't have to spend your life on a quest to find someone to help you? When you have Christ, He is all the help you need. He has been there all the time. Never forget to turn to Him, and never let anyone have His place. If you do, you will always be disappointed. He is the One who gives you the power to change. With Him on your side you will always survive. You are empowered by the presence of God.

The feeling of powerlessness can be depressing and create habits of sin. It can cause you to sink in your morality and your character because you feel imprisoned. You would be amazed at the number of people who have decided that they have no options or windows in their

lives. They have entombed themselves with guilt. They have embalmed themselves with regret; they exist in a constant state of decomposition.

You will see them on the job. You will see them in the streets. You will even find them in church. Their painted nails are banging keys on the computer. They are dressed in business suits or doctor's frocks, but they are dead. These will be the women you will find with smiling lips but vacant eyes. The glow has gone out of their cheeks. The bells have ceased to jingle in their voice. They are mannequins, stuck on the stage of life. They are all dressed up and going nowhere. They have rocked their faith to sleep in the cradle of depression, and they are reaping the bitter rewards of negative thinking.

Hear me today: You are not imprisoned; you are empowered. Take control of your circumstances in Jesus' name and arise. You're a daughter of the King, and you can arise by His power without hesitation. Knowing this sets you free.

Like Dorothy, you had the power all the time, even if you didn't know it. It's the knowledge of your liberty that the enemy wants to steal from you. He cannot take away the *power* to be free. So he tries to steal the *knowledge* of your freedom. He really laughs when he sees you entrapped behind an open door. There you are crying and frustrated, tormented and afraid. The fact is that two thousand years ago your God unlocked the door, and you can walk through it at will. You just don't know it!

No wonder the Bible says, "How beautiful are the feet of them that preach the gospel" (Rom. 10:15, KJV). Preaching to you doesn't set you free; it just announces to you that you are free. It is a declaration of independence. It is God's word showing you step by step how to click your heels and get away from the enemy! Click them now. You have been in that state too long. Click them in the name of Jesus.

That's right. You have the power to get away from the past and get on with your life. Click, click, click! Just when the enemy thought he had you, click, and you are gone.

Moving from imprisonment to empowerment takes some people longer than others. It helps when you have had good, strong childhood affirmation. But even if you didn't, you don't have to limit your future merely because of voids in your past. Close those chapters in your life and write new ones. Even women who were loved, affirmed and nurtured as children may not be exempt from challenges. Sometimes all that you have been provided does not fill the void. It simply doesn't sink in. Many times it is given, and we fail to receive what is being offered. Regardless of the reason why you are in a state, what is most important is that you escape. Leah had some struggles and didn't have strong childhood affirmation, but in the midst of her dysfunction she developed a functional relationship with God.

Her father didn't value her. And God only knows what happened to her mother. She was betrayed by her father, who used her as a consolation prize to Jacob (Gen. 29:17-23). Laban thought she was second class and dumped her off on Jacob. If he had been a wise father, he would have known that Leah was gifted. She wasn't gifted in the same way her sister was, but she was gifted just the same. His other daughter, Rachel, was beautiful. Leah wasn't what you would traditionally call beautiful, yet she had strength, and God wanted to use her in a mighty way.

Girls, just because you are not gifted like someone else doesn't mean that you are not gifted. God never made a worthless child. Leah had worth. It just wasn't the kind of worth that was obvious to her father. She found herself entangled with the same kind of a man for a husband that she had for a father. He wasn't very kind to her, but that wasn't anything new. In fact, it was familiar. Almost like a

magnet draws metal, we can seemingly draw similar circumstances into our lives. Thank God, He knows how to make the negatives turn to positives. He can wean you from your past mistakes.

When we think of the term *weaning* we think in terms of mothers — and mothers do wean their young. Even animal mothers wean their young. But I want you to know that the Father also weans His young. He weans us through life's circumstances. He weans us until we get the strength to make proper choices. He knows how to bring us to a state of security where we cease to be so dependent on others and their affirmation.

The weaning process is not easy. Many times you will have to be weaned in your flesh by the power in your spirit. You will have to allow the Spirit of God to control you to the point where He can help you through the process of being weaned from some things and habits that you don't need. He can nourish you at the better place He has prepared for you.

The weaning process is painful because you want what you want the way you are used to getting it. It takes great faith to know that you can give up what you had and get better than you experienced before. Please don't limit the concept of weaning to just people. It may be a job you need to be weaned from. It may be a city, a ministry or a poor career choice — a limiting circumstance that has brought your life to a screeching halt. The Father weans us from what we thought we had to have in order to give us what He has for us. His plans are so much better than ours that it is worth the pain to make the switch.

> But that we write unto them, that they abstain from pollutions of idols, and from fornication, and from things strangled, and from blood (Acts 15:20, KJV).

Leah starts out birthing babies to impress someone who

isn't impressed. She is being blessed, but she isn't enjoying it; she is only using the blessing to get the attention of someone who has become an idol in her life. My little ones, be careful that you abstain from idols. Acts 15:20 reminds us that the Old Testament forbade the saints of old from even eating meats that were offered up to idols. They were considered unclean.

In our modern times we think idols and their offerings are obsolete, but that is not true! Today the idols have taken on a disguise. They are camouflaged and arrayed in socially acceptable concepts and ideas. Let's disrobe them and expose their danger. Idols are the things you worship, the things to which you yield your strength. They are false gods.

Oh, don't be coy. I know that most of us have no physical shrines in our homes, no graven images that we bow before. Yet many Christians are living for and serving things that are false gods and have dedicated their attention, their energy and their efforts to these unworthy images. Don't you realize you can worship things by paying them too much attention? You can worship them by dedicating your life to impressing them. You can worship them by allowing their opinion to determine your self-worth or esteem. That thing is an idol in your life.

You have shed tears over it. You have birthed blessings that you have not enjoyed because you did a right thing for a wrong reason. That is what Leah did. She was birthing sons but for the wrong reason. She was trying to win Jacob with her successes instead of thanking God that He had given her an area of success to balance the many failures. God often gives us successes to balance the bitterness of failures! Leah missed out on a real experience with God, a time of thanksgiving and communion, because her strength was sapped away through idolatry.

And when the Lord saw that Leah was hated, he opened her womb: but Rachel was barren. And Leah conceived, and bare a son; and she called his name Reuben: for she said, Surely the Lord hath looked upon my affliction; now therefore my husband will love me. And she conceived again, and bare a son; and said, Because the Lord hath heard that I was hated, he hath therefore given me this son also: and she called his name Simeon. And she conceived again, and bare a son; and said, Now this time will my husband be joined unto me, because I have born him three sons: therefore was his name called Levi. And she conceived again, and bare a son; and she said, Now will I praise the Lord: therefore she called his name Judah; and left bearing (Gen. 29:31-35, KJV).

Finally, after a series of births, three to be exact, she comes to a state of weaning. She has reached a degree of maturity, though she will struggle in this area again. Winning Jacob's love will always be an area of vulnerability for her. She has refocused her attention on the Giver of life and the Healer of hearts. To a degree these first three children were offered up on the altar of their mother's broken heart. They were an offering that Leah gave to the idol she couldn't reject within her own damaged life.

After this she births Judah. He is the fourth child, the one after the third, three being the number of resurrection. She has been resurrected, and she testifies in verse 35, "Now will I praise the Lord." *Judah* means "praise." You cannot praise and honor God for what He has given you until you have been weaned from the idols you have lived for in the past!

Now, can we confront the Jacob in your life? Is there an idol, the thing in your life that has stolen your attention

and emotions from a God who keeps blessing you? Have you missed the sweet taste of God's favor because you took the successes that He gave you and paraded them before others whose minds you wanted to change? Have you idolized a place, a thing, a job, a school or some other god that has stolen your interest and a major portion of your energy? If so, don't be ashamed — we have all done it, but few have the courage to confront their idols. They hide them in blankets and carry them with them.

Is there an area in your life where the Holy Spirit has nudged you as you read this? Is there an area or issue that you have allowed to become an idol? It may be an ex-husband. It may be a childhood rivalry with your sister. It could be the result of burning, painful words that scalded your heart and left you blistered inside!

This may be an area that God needs to heal in your life. I join you in faith and prayer, and I break the spirit of idolatry over your life. You will live for the Lord and no one else! I agree with you in prayer that God in His mercy would restore unto you the joy of your salvation. Lord, restore to Your daughter the joy of having You, the joy of being at peace within. I rebuke that spirit that drives and torments her — stealing precious moments from her. In Jesus' name, be loosed!

If you have been feeling like you were being driven and not led, if you have been compelled by some need to prove something or validate yourself, stop it now. If you are a Christian, you were validated two thousand years ago. On the cross of Calvary our Father set us free. You are not to be driven or compelled, controlled or dominated, not by a person, a goal or even your own flesh. He died to set you free.

I remember counseling a young lady who was headstrong and driven. She was having a terrible time handling some of the Bible's teaching on submission as it relates to

marriage. She was engaged, and she wanted to be sure that she set some ground rules for her husband. She was afraid of being mistreated and unhappy.

She was concerned about the word *obey* in her wedding ceremony. I told her taking the words out of the ceremony is far easier than taking them out of the Word of God. Even if we removed them from the ceremony, which I would not do, we cannot remove them from the Word of God.

> You wives must submit to your husbands' leadership in the same way you submit to the Lord. For a husband is in charge of his wife in the same way Christ is in charge of his body the church. (He gave his very life to take care of it and be its Savior!) So you wives must willingly obey your husbands in everything, just as the church obeys Christ (Eph. 5:22-24, TLB).

Of course, the Bible balances its teaching on submission by telling the men to "love your wives just as Christ also loved the church" (v. 25, NAS). Just the same, she was annoyed with me and infuriated. I calmly explained that the Bible is just laying down the guidelines.

"It isn't fair," she complained. "The man has all the rights!"

"No," I replied. "That is not true. The reason the Bible describes the qualities of the man as well is that God has given the woman the first right of marriage."

She said, "What right is that?"

I responded, "The right to choose."

If you forfeit that right, you are foolish. You have the right to choose the kind of man to whom you want to be submitted. Woe unto the woman who hasn't been healed and says yes to a man because his treatment to her is familiar and not biblical. You want the God kind of man, not just

a good man. No, he is not God, but he should be the kind of man who has decided he wants to love you as God says he should. You, in response to that choice, should honor him by not living in rebellion and contention.

In closing this chapter, at the risk of sounding like an overly protective father, I want to warn you to be careful what and whom you choose. I want to warn you against basing a permanent decision on a temporary feeling. Don't choose for lust. Don't choose for fortune and fame. Don't choose because of notoriety. All these things will fade. Choose the God kind of man if you are going to marry. And choose no man to serve like a king who hasn't honored you as his queen. You will always be Daddy's girls, but you ought to be your husband's queen!

Chapter ❤ *Six*

Daughterhood, Motherhood and Beyond

$\mathcal{I}$ know you've been wondering when it was going to come. Well, here it is. This is the advice that fathers give to their daughters. It is the kind of investment from which you will draw dividends at another stage of life. It may not prepare you for the details of life, but it will strengthen you to endure the generalized attacks that come against most women as they pass through life from day to day.

It is a word to the wise and a thought to the thinker, a morsel of food reserved for a time when perhaps my lips

will be silenced and my fingers stilled by the grand finale we all face. After years of ministering and counseling ladies whose hearts have been broken by the changing winds of the seasons of life, I thought I ought to leave a grain of wheat to be shared by those who will face their own times of change and adversity.

It is the kind of advice a businessman seeks from his broker. The investment may not pay at this moment, but take it, put it away and wait. It will gather and accrue interest for a day when you need it most. I bequeath to you the benefit of my experience and interest drawn from the fragments of pain that many have left in my office after counseling, prayers and tears. I bequeath this information to you in hope that you will be forewarned and thereby forearmed against the plot and plan of the enemy, who is forever planning our demise.

Changes, Changes and More Changes

The Lord is exalted; for he dwelleth on high: he hath filled Zion with judgment and righteousness. And wisdom and knowledge shall be the stability of thy times, and strength of salvation: the fear of the Lord is his treasure (Is. 33:5-6, KJV).

Life will bring many changes. By the time you become accustomed to school you will face college. By the time you learn to ignore the constant distractions imposed upon you by students inviting you to be a participant in their unique brand of madness, it will be time for graduation.

If you choose the path that leads to marriage, you will suddenly find yourself a wife. What that means varies, based upon whom you marry. You will write your own definition of marriage when you select your partner. I caution you to select wisely. Even if you survive a bad decision, the

fruit of the mistake will greatly affect your sense of well-being and self-esteem. Do not allow the loneliness of youth to tempt you into the emptiness of selecting someone whose maturity has been fragmented and commitment fractured. I can assure you that marriage is for grown women and grown men. It is not wrong to be a child. But it is wrong for children to play the games of the mature.

What I am trying to tell you is life has a middle name, and the name is change. If you are going to thrive in life, you must be liquid enough to flow with change. Rigid, inflexible women are broken and destroyed because they fail to develop elasticity for change. It is a great blessing when you understand that life is full of change. Change is unavoidable: Anything that grows will change. These are the seasons of life. Your beauty will change. It may not diminish, but it will certainly alter. But what is beauty anyway? It's not the opinion of someone whose eyes cannot see beyond the cosmetics. Each definition of beauty varies from person to person. What sayeth thou?

If you are like your mother, you will also birth children. When you have children, hold them, love them, care for them, empower them. But understand that you are only temporary stewards. They belong to God. They will grow up and leave. They were not meant to be grasped or clung to as if you could freeze a moment. No, moments cannot be frozen, but you will be allowed to hold memories. If you are good at mothering, you will hold the memories and release the child. If you cannot do that, you will destroy the memories by corrupting the relationship between you and the little chick whose development has outgrown the shell of your parenting.

I want to spend time dealing with this because many women come close to losing their relationships with their children. They feel betrayed by the growth of the child that they trained. They have trained the children to be productive

and then have failed to prepare themselves for that growth — not just the growth of the body but also the growth of the person, the development of personalities and preferences. They feel that their children are belligerent when in truth many of the children are just independent. Of course there are children who grow to be calloused. I pray that you will be spared the disappointment of that experience. But even if your parenting goes well, there will still be moments when you see your children slipping through your fingers like grains of sand. For many mothers who once struggled to wean the child from tender breasts, it is later a struggle to wean the mother from the child!

> But Hannah went not up; for she said unto her husband, I will not go up until the child be weaned, and then I will bring him, that he may appear before the Lord, and there abide for ever (1 Sam. 1:22, KJV).

Letting go is especially painful when you allow your relationship with your child to become cluttered like an attic stuffed with things that belong somewhere else. Often there are misplaced passions dumped on the child to compensate for loneliness in other areas. Because there was no place to put them, they were shoved into the attic. Often it is love that should have been invested in a spouse, but there was no spouse there or no capacity in the spouse to be loved. So the love was dumped on a child. This is not a healthy love; it is obsessive.

There is a great deal of difference between a natural love and affection for our children and an inordinate obsession that develops to compensate for emptiness in other areas. Eventually the mother is just putting off the inevitable. It is a subconscious delay many mothers use to avoid developing a healthy self-image. They must have a cause. They must be martyrs who give their lives on behalf of another.

Tragically, when the child leaves, it will seem to the mother that she has been forsaken again. This simply is not true. The child was on loan to you.

Every good mother, sooner or later, must understand she is denied ownership; she is merely granted stewardship. This is so important. One of the most sensitive times you will face as a mother is the weaning of yourself from your child. For some women it is less stressful than for others. It will be easier if you maintain some contact with your own personhood aside from the role you play as a mother to a child. If not, you will have perfected a role that will come to an end.

I don't want you to be left with big pots and pans hanging on the wall that you can't use because the ones you fed have gone. Greater still, I don't want you to be one of those mothers whose anger and hostility pours out upon a child who is becoming increasingly frustrated. The hostility coming from that mother many times is just a shield for the broken heart of a woman who feels rejected and betrayed by a child whose only crime was developing a life of his own.

Keep the attic clean. Do not give your children the part of your heart that they were not meant to hold. Do not dump your pain, frustration or even your affection upon them more lavishly than a good mother should. If you do, you will find yourself bribing your children to stay with you, and that will cripple them.

You might say, I see the problem, but what is the answer? I am glad you asked. You need to develop other interests. It is important that you do not lose your sense of personhood. Don't stop valuing yourself and your needs. The Word of God doesn't teach us to be selfish, but it does admonish us to love others as we love ourselves (Matt. 19:19). If we do not have a healthy self-esteem, we either do not love others or we love them as a way of ignoring ourselves.

Keep your mind fresh and your spirit crisp by having expectations that go beyond the goals you have for your children. You cannot live your life for a second time through their bodies. They have the right to learn and grow, fail and survive even as you did. You can guide them and gird them, but be careful you don't become a manipulator who cannot let go of a past relationship because it met you at the point of your personal need!

> And she vowed a vow, and said, O Lord of hosts, if thou wilt indeed look on the affliction of thine handmaid, and remember me, and not forget thine handmaid, but wilt give unto thine handmaid a man child, then I will give him unto the Lord all the days of his life, and there shall no razor come upon his head (1 Sam. 1:11, KJV).

Hannah meets a prerequisite that is a foundation of healthy parenting. She enters into the covenant of motherhood understanding herself to be a steward. Her faith in God is proven by her willingness to give her children back to the God who gave them to her. It is easier to give them back if you understand from the beginning they aren't yours to keep. But it is not impossible in the middle of your life to gather your faith and turn children over to God in later years. You have deposited in them all that you can. That is all that you can do. Understand that the same God who protected you and brought you through is able to keep them.

My advice for you, daughter, is to be prepared for change. Everything will do it — people, circumstances and situations. It helps when you know that from the beginning. Listen to the words of the hymn that brought your father through the storms and the tempestuous changes of life:

Time is filled with swift transitions.
Naught of earth unmoved can stand.
Build your hopes on things eternal.
And hold to God's unchanging hand.

There is no escaping it. The firm breasts that were once small lumps will inflate with child-rearing and deflate in later years. Eyes that burned with fervent love will mellow and alter in time. I don't mean that love doesn't last. I simply suggest that even surviving love changes in its expression and its manifestation. It survives in various forms. You must be a person who is willing to see that change as a positive and explore each stage as if God has a present locked inside of it for you, because He does. He will show you the many splendors of life if your eyes do not become too affixed on one aspect of its radiance.

If a couple remains married for fifty or sixty years, it is not because the husband sees his wife as if she stayed the same as on their wedding day. She doesn't look the same, and he doesn't either. They don't love the same. They don't touch the same. It takes them longer to do what they used to do easily. They are together like voyagers exploring the experience of each stage. Beneath leathery skin and wrinkled eyes there are burning embers of wisdom and experience. They still know love, but they express it in changing forms. As it is with them, so it is with change in your own life, whether it is the independence of your children, a new job or a move.

I have sat behind my desk and felt the fear leaping from the hearts of women whose anger poorly camouflaged the struggles they were having with changing times. Some were very spiritual, but even that can become a cloak for denial. There are women who bury themselves in the business of caring for others' needs to escape the void in their own lives. When those persons for whom they care leave, they

must face the naked emptiness they hid from for years.

These things are not easily confronted. You have to take a large dose of honesty to even get close to accepting that you have turned a person into an attic for your collection of misplaced affections and attentions. It is amazing how the enemy will subtly rob you of new experiences and the freshness that we all need. Many people are depressed and bored because when God gets ready to bring new experiences, they reject them and cleave to what is familiar even if it is not exciting!

My advice to you, my daughters, is to never forget how to let go. Sometimes it will be people; sometimes it will be things; sometimes it will be letting go of a moment that you can never repeat. If you have ever lost a loved one you can relate to this analogy. Nothing challenges our ability to let go like death. It wrenches from our hands a loved one to whom we would cling forever if we could. When you stand over a casket that is being lowered in the ground, truth slaps you in the face. The person you loved is gone. How could they go and leave you like that? However painful, death is a part of life.

For Christians, death is a portal that enables us to move from one realm of existence into another. Eventually death will knock on the door no matter who we are. It helps a little to know that he will come. When he does, God will give you grace to accept what cannot be changed. That same grace will empower you as you learn to cope with changes among the living. Grace empowers us to continue and experience with God's help. Why don't you ask Him for the grace you need to accept the things that you cannot change? When He gives it to you, get on with your life.

Each experience has its own value if you do not close your eyes to where you are, trying foolishly to be where you have already been. I know life can feel terribly unstable and vulnerable when you accept change. But I am so glad

God ever remains the same. He is the stability that enables us to adjust to the variables of life.

If you are reading this and you recognize areas in your life where you have been guilty of resisting change, stop right where you are and allow God to cleanse your heart from the fear of change. Know in your spirit that something good is going to come out of it. Take it in stride and start planning ways that you can enjoy where you are. Maybe you have been neglecting your children, husband or job. You want to go back to the past. But you are also missing the good things that God has prepared for you today.

Our faith teaches us to trust God. He doesn't change, but His methods of ministering to you will change over and over again. Do not worry. He will give you what you need when you need it. He may not bring it the same way twice, but what do you care how He does it as long as you know He does it? Leave the "hows" in the hands of the great One who is able to control the circumstances in your life. Repent from manipulating those with whom you associate. Let them go. You have no right to hold anyone a prisoner in the jail cell of your fears, not even yourself. Let yourself go. You have been imprisoned from what God wants to give you most, a new experience in Christ Jesus!

> Remember ye not the former things, neither con-
> sider the things of old. Behold, I will do a new
> thing; now it shall spring forth; shall ye not know
> it? I will even make a way in the wilderness, and
> rivers in the desert (Is. 43:18-19, KJV).

In short, dear daughters, there seems to be a struggle in the hearts of many women who wrestle with changing roles, changing times and changing relationships. Much has been said about the changes in life but not nearly enough in regard to the maternal heart that has unfortunately allowed itself to be defined purely by its relationship with

children. The children become adults, their needs change and they are gone. But the woman who nurtured them must always remember she is more than their last assignment. God has sustained you in this life because you are needed. Perhaps it is not a need that requires a clean bandage on an old cut. It may not be a need that requires a quick trip to the PTA meeting to settle a dispute. But you are needed. Be careful that you do not hold those around you captive. You must love enough to let go.

It takes faith to let go of the former things. Many cling to the past because they are convinced that their better days are behind them. This attitude leads to great depression. If you can accept the challenge to which God is calling you and realize there are new levels of love and life before you, it will be great. Take some of that stuff you jammed in the attic and move it to some place where it can be used. Renovate your life with love and hope and release bitterness. A woman who can move on is invincible. She may affect her nation like Esther or lead a people like Deborah. She may nurture someone else's child at the breast of her experience as Naomi did Ruth. She may be able to serve her church like Anna. Whatever your next assignment in life, you will miss it if you worship the past and yearn for yesterday. Let it go!

The greatest tragedy is that many mothers end up with resentful children who feel smothered and angry because they are made to feel guilty for growing up! Preserve what you have with your children by allowing the relationship to change in your hand. The caterpillar has been fed in the cocoon of your teaching and has come forth a butterfly. It will never crawl again. It will never need what it once needed, but in every flap of its lovely wings there is a tribute to the cocoon that allowed it the grace of change.

Your authority has changed. You move from an authoritative sovereign to an advisor. That is not disrespect but

development! Your word may not be law, and they may not wear the color you think they should. But if you respect yesterday's child and recognize that he has become today's adult, he will always love you for the tremendous contribution you made to that independence.

One of the greatest challenges of this adjustment is the redefining of boundaries. During this time the child must have adequate training to understand that he needs independence without being disrespectful. Young people struggle to know their role and perhaps will blunder in the process of attaining their goals. But didn't most of us stumble into destiny? Children cannot exist as extensions of their parents. The weaning process can be challenging for all concerned.

> And when they saw him, they were amazed: and his mother said unto him, Son, why hast thou thus dealt with us? behold, thy father and I have sought thee sorrowing. And he said unto them, How is it that ye sought me? wist ye not that I must be about my Father's business? (Luke 2:48-49, KJV).

Jesus returned home with his mother and continued to submit to her. But the Scriptures say that from that time he increased "in wisdom and stature, and in favor with God and man" (Luke 2:52, KJV). It is important to recognize that He did not disassociate from His mother, whose loyalty followed Him all the way to the cross. Although their roles changed and He became increasingly independent, His love and care for her continued even to His thirty-third year and the final moments of life. She was still His mother!

> Now there stood by the cross of Jesus his mother, and his mother's sister, Mary the wife of Cleophas, and Mary Magdalene. When Jesus therefore saw his mother, and the disciple standing by, whom he

loved, he saith unto his mother, Woman, behold thy son! Then saith he to the disciple, Behold thy mother! And from that hour that disciple took her unto his own home (John 19:25-27, KJV).

There are two things that are really important if we are to go through the metamorphosis of relationships without destroying the fragrance of love. The first issue is the adult child's willingness to envelop the mother with affirmation and respect that will not lend itself to intimidation. We all wonder, Will I be loved when I am not needed? The truth of the matter is the need is still there, but the areas of need have changed. Affirm your mother by guiding her to areas where she will always be needed. This brings me to the second equally crucial issue. The mother must have faith to let go of the past relationship and lay hold of the future without allowing fear to diminish the warm embers of maternal wisdom that exist in the inner sanctum of her heart. You can develop a fresh relationship with your daughter or even your son.

Avoid the temptation to attack the people who are a part of your children's adult life. Many mothers make the mistake of releasing the role of mother and replacing it with the role of judge. She becomes a critic of other persons who have influence with her adult children. No one is attracted to a critic, and without knowing it she pushes her loved ones away. You have too much invested in the relationship to lose your head. Whether you are wrestling with jealousy or you genuinely do not approve, prayer is a better choice than bickering and nagging!

Remember Naomi, who stood by Ruth, her daughter-in-law. Her wisdom and gentle encouragement gave strength and grace to the young girl she influenced. Ruth and Naomi shared life, love and intimate secrets without Naomi judging, criticizing or dominating Ruth. Ultimately Ruth

became committed to the God of Naomi. The greatest witness we can have is the presence of grace. Be gracious and you will see God move in your life!

Your children would be extremely ill-equipped for life if they had grown physically but had not developed their own opinions and uniqueness. You are always entitled to your opinion, but once you have said it, release them to make their own decision. Respect their choices and support them as best you can. Do not allow the enemy to rob you of the riches of your investment in your children. It would be silly to lose all you have invested in someone over one issue!

Mary, the mother of Jesus, didn't understand her son. His decisions led Him to a cross. Yet she supported Him to the end. You must be wise! If not, you will create a cold war which will leave you alone with bitterness and sad memories. Your hostility will cause you to be left with Thanksgiving turkeys with no one to eat them and holidays without family. It is not worth it. Back up and pray!

> For of this sort are they which creep into houses, and lead captive silly women laden with sins, led away with divers lusts, ever learning, and never able to come to the knowledge of the truth (2 Tim. 3:6-7, KJV).

As I close this chapter — this manual for my daughters and all daughters and mothers — realize that time brings change. Change is not always an enemy. It can be God's way of saying enough is enough. He will promote you from one task to another. If you can remain flexible and face the changes of life with the assurance of God, you will win. It is God's desire to make you a wise woman.

My daughters, for the many changes you will face on all levels of life, I recommend Jesus. He does not change. He is an unchanging God in a rapidly changing world. If you are going to survive you must learn how to accept change,

whether that change involves your marriage, your children or other areas. Do not be tormented by something that was wonderful at one time. Know when it is time to have new discoveries.

Even in the cold crispness of winter there will be sunny days. Early in the morning when icicles hang from eaves there are still the glowing, glistening rays of morning sun. Though the wind has howled all night, and the gusts beat vehemently against the house, there will be a morning. Expect it in every season of life. Get up every morning and throw aside the curtain of doubt. Brush past the foggy films that would cloud your eyes from seeing what is right in front of you and embrace expectancy. It is the breaking of a new day. It is the establishing of fresh options. The birds wake up singing in the morning.

Now I know no two days will be the same. They were not designed to be duplicated. Each one is a new expression of a multifaceted God whose being could not be defined in just one circumstance. Every day we will behold a new wonder of His glory. A splendor, a splice, a sliver of His radiance will dispel the fear of the future. Now, stop crying and fretting over this and that. You will create your own rain.

Get up rejoicing in a day that someone missed. While you slept someone gasped a final sigh and slipped from time into eternity without seeing this day. But you are still here. This is God's gift to you. From the God who cares enough to give the very best, He gave you today. Enjoy it. It is yours. There will never be another moment like this one.

Reinhold Niebuhr said it better than anyone I have ever heard: "O God, give us serenity to accept what cannot be changed, courage to change what should be changed, and wisdom to distinguish the one from the other." He will do it. It is not just a prayer if you pray it. It will become an answer that presents you before the thundering applause of those who love you. They will respect you because, dear daughters, the older a woman becomes the wiser she is expected to become! Do not disappoint us — we are all waiting for the curtain to slide out of the way. The world is waiting to see how you will handle this. My advice to you as a father and as a friend is simple: Just blow their minds!

Chapter Seven

Some Things Nurtured,
Some Things Neutered

𝒯 wish you could have seen what I saw watching your mother with our children. It's a beauty that is more radiant than bursts of sunlight. It has always fascinated me that she found the grace to sit up all night with fevers and rock heavy babies in weary arms without complaining. I fear that mothers of her magnitude are on a decline, so I want to share some of the vibrance I have seen as she paced the floor at night holding each of you.

I am a fairly resourceful man, and I have done some

night duty helping as I could to ease the discomfort of some affliction that attempted to capture my children in its clutches. But as night ebbed on, sleep would imprison me. I would drag my remains back into the bedroom and, like a falling tree, collapse into the waiting bed and not awake until morning. To my amazement, your mother would be up. Sometimes she had been up all night. She can rock a child longer than the strongest man in the world. She has the strength of ten men when it comes to her children.

I learned long ago not to compete with her maternal instincts. They are sharp and keen. She has the eye of an eagle. She can look at any of us and tell at a glance when we are not well. She notices puffiness in the eye or a multitude of other symptoms that go unobserved by others. It is absolutely uncanny to me.

I have known her to cook, clothe and feed all of us while she was staggering with a fever. I am convinced that she doesn't get sick. Or if she does it must not be the kind of sickness that I get. When I get sick the whole room becomes a crib. I almost want to stick my thumb in my mouth. I want my mother, my wife and at least ten highly skilled nurses. I check my last will and testament when I have a cold and look over my insurance policies if I have the flu. No matter what I do, it must be done from a warm bed accompanied by a bowl of chicken noodle soup and a glass of ice cold ginger ale.

When your mother gets the same bug, generally she shrugs it off, slips on her house shoes, starts coffee with one hand and wakes up the children with the other. She is bionic. She can rock the baby, answer the phone, lay out my clothes and curl her hair at the same time without blinking. How is this possible? I do not know. All I know is that God seems to give good women the grace to continue under pressure. I am amazed at some of the things that pass for mothering today.

Even my own mother could bake a birthday cake while talking on the phone — without a mixer. I can still see her robust arms trembling as she creamed the four rigid sticks of butter into the mountain of sugar that she had placed in the bowl and beat with a spoon turned flat down in the bowl. Not only that, she could heat food without a microwave. I remember her cooking many roasts on top of a broken stove that should have been thrown away.

Without much help she could take twenty-five dollars and a bus ticket and go to the grocery store with three children clutching her cotton dress. She would come back with a week's worth of groceries and cook the dinner before five without packaged food or processed meats.

I am so thankful I have seen real parenting. These counterfeit mothers who toss their babies into open trash cans as if they were discarding old shoes may be female, but they are not women. Let's continue our heritage of excellence in parenting. If you do not have that heritage, let it start with you. We need our families healed and restored.

What is more touching than to see a mother clutching a child in the warm arms of maternal love? Have you ever seen a baby snuggle down into the soft, pillowy bosom of its mother and smile softly as it hears the ticking of her loving heart? It is the rhythm of life. What a wonderfully natural thing it is to see women of all races and religions loving their children. The African woman holding her baby has the same sparkle in her eyes that her Chinese sister does. From Hawaii to London, Russia to Italy, there are certain feelings that transcend culture. This is the love from which truth is spawned. We are all very alike when it comes to the essentials of life. We need, we love, we touch, we give! What else can we do but love what God has allowed us to parent?

I realize that as I share the supremacy of women as it

relates to child care that I have overlooked many men who have assumed the position of single parents; to each of them I quickly bow in admiration. You are princes, and God will bless you for your loving demonstration to all men that it can be done if it becomes necessary. Yet there is something unique about a woman's natural ability to nurture.

In the case of the Shunammite woman whose son fell into the arms of his father, complaining about his head, it was his mother who refused to accept the impending death of her child. She saddled an animal and rode to the man of God and demanded that he raise up the now-dead child. She completely disregarded all of her intelligence. She knew the child was dead; she just refused to accept it. She held on to the child. She was so convinced he would live that she would not bury him (2 Kin. 4:8-37).

She is no different from Rizpah, a mother who pitched her tent on a rock to guard the putrid, decaying flesh of her dead sons whose bodies were hanging. She endured the stench for many days until she got the attention of the king who finally arranged for the bodies to be buried (2 Sam. 21:8-11). What of Mary and the other women who ran down to the tomb expecting to find the dead, decaying body of Jesus, while the disciples were shut up in a room for fear of the Jews?

In short, there is something about women that we must discuss. When a woman is pregnant, she shares her food and oxygen with a baby she has never seen, much less known. Her warm hands stroke her bulging abdomen as she reaches out to a baby who cannot see her, yet there is a bond that exists before birth. Her strength is shared; her mineral and protein supplies begin to serve two guests at one table. Her cord carries life to a child whose every need is dependent upon her for fulfillment. Her tender breasts collect milk as they become the place where the baby looks for food. He need not depart from her — his needs can all be met in her arms. She touches him; she changes him; she feeds him.

Men could not create a machine that is as multifaceted as a mother. What else do you know that can feed, clothe, touch, love, provide intimacy and affection, food and training? All these needs are met for the child without ever leaving that one spot. This is the place of provision. It is the place of excellence.

As is always the case, however, the things that make us very good and very functional, if introverted, make us dysfunctional and depraved. That same nurturing instinct that enables a mother to hold a child all night without regard for her own feelings or physical needs can cause that woman to cleave to a relationship that is diseased or hold on to an issue that is dead and decomposed. Many women are such nurturers that they find it difficult to let go, even when they must.

It is dangerous when a woman holds on to things that should be released. I have counseled women whose hearts have been broken by someone who has been gone out of their lives for years; yet they find it difficult to dismiss the experiences and move on. Rarely will you meet a man who is enamored for years with someone who has gone out of his life. Men are not much for sitting around waiting for someone to come back.

Now, dear daughters, don't think that men don't have feelings, because we do have feelings. We don't always articulate them as easily as you do, but we have them nevertheless. It is just that we are not by nature nurturers, and we have a tendency to erase issues more easily than some women do.

Perhaps that is why the Holy Spirit comes right out and challenges men who have had the new birth to nourish the wife as if she were his own body (Eph. 5:29). This is a charge that only the Holy Spirit can give, because by nature

in our old state we are not nurturers. The strength of Paul's argument rests on the appeal for men to care for their own bodies. Well, sir, your wife is in fact your body!

Admittedly, this is a challenge that God helps men to perform, but women are by nature nurturers. Their struggle is often in the area of submission, so the Holy Spirit challenges women to submit (Eph. 5:22). Had the woman been submitted to her husband she would have referred the serpent in the garden to him, her covering. As the church, the submitted bride of Christ, we are told to submit ourselves unto God, resist the devil and he will flee (James 4:7). The submitted vessel gains strength to resist. When the enemy meets with real resistance, he will flee. The whole concept hinges on the fact that the battle is not mine, but it belongs to the One who covers me!

The Holy Spirit establishes within the woman the nurturing spirit that will not allow her to push away her young but to nurse them patiently and care for them. Doesn't it make you angry to see how the enemy always wants to pervert good for evil? You see, Satan cannot create. He is not God. He has to use what is already created. He perverts, corrupts and even disrupts, but he cannot create. The wise woman learns his devices. Once you learn what he is trying to do, appropriate your strengths for positive usage and stop him from seducing you into nurturing what needs to be neutered!

Nurturing a problem not only means you keep it, it also implies that you are feeding it. It is drawing your strength from you, just as a child has no way of getting food in the mother's womb except from her. The enemy cannot live in a blood-washed, regenerated spirit. The enemy can only thrive in your mind if you let him live off of your old memories and fears. He is a leech that is depending upon your umbilical cord for survival. You ought to cut the cord and watch your fears starve to death.

Like Rizpah, who would not leave her dead sons, you have to be careful that you are not hanging around dead issues and keeping company with things that ought to be put to death. Rizpah was being faithful to her children, but some of you are hanging around some issue that isn't yours. It is the enemy seeking whom he may devour (1 Pet. 5:8)!

Chapter Eight

An Enemy Hath Done This!

I have often asked women, "Haven't you ever wondered where all of this pain is coming from?" Their situation reminds me of one of Jesus' parables.

> So the servants of the householder came and said unto him, Sir, didst not thou sow good seed in thy field? from whence then hath it tares? He said unto them, An enemy hath done this (Matt. 13:27-28, KJV).

These women seem not to realize that Satan sowed tares into their good fields. By doing this he used their nurturing instincts against them. Some of them had wasted years of productivity trying to recapture and revive something that wasn't even worth all of the milk (resources) they were using to nurture it. They should have cut the cord years ago.

In the modern drug rehabilitation programs, they call the person who is involved in a relationship with an addict the *enabler*. Enablers are not necessarily addicted to the drug, but they have not learned to cut the cord between themselves and the addict. Consequently, they are drawn into the madness of the other person. Although they hate the addiction, they unintentionally make it possible for the addict to continue what he or she is doing. They have become an enabler.

In that same way, you can become a nurturer of something that is depleting you. It is wearing you down, and yet you keep pouring into it. You pour emotion and attention. You pour out your energy, and, worst of all, you sacrifice your future to an idol that is not worthy of your worship. You are nurturing something that needs to be neutered.

"How can I separate from this person?" you ask. The answer is simple; you don't cut off the person. You simply, as an act of your will, make a decision about your lifestyle. How do you want to live your life? That is the question that each of us must ask. And after asking the question, we must not complain about the answer. We can choose how we want to live, and then we must live with the choices we make. There are times that we must determine whether we really want to go deeper into the valley of pain just for the benefit of saying, I am not alone. It is saying, I reject this lifestyle. That doesn't require rejecting a person unless that person considers the lifestyle more important

than you are. In that case, the other person made the choice.

Many women find it difficult to confront these issues because, as a nurturer, they always put others' comfort above their own. It sounds unselfish, but many times it is just a nice dress scantily covering a low self-esteem!

Let's go deeper, because many of the detrimental things that are being nurtured are not people at all. They are issues and struggles, bondages and fears that are still growing through the choices of the one who nurtures them. You can nurture a fear that no one even knows you are harboring. Daughters, there may come a time when you become aware you are harboring some negative feelings or attitudes. That is understandable, but look a little closer. Many people with these feelings often inadvertently feed the feelings. They rehash over and over again the kind of stinking thinking that will enslave them and rob them of the virtue they need to arise.

You must know when it is time to neuter the things Satan is using to sap your strength from you! Have you noticed that when women are pregnant their skin loses color? They become weak and dizzy because the baby is sapping their strength. If you are carrying old pain, old scars, dead relationships or even a torch for someone who has moved on with his life, I counsel you to abort that thing that is draining your life and blurring your vision. You are a nurturing being, but you can neuter that thing. Let it go, in Jesus' name! The Word literally instructs us to cast our cares on Him (1 Pet. 5:7)! Now, no one casts anything that they care about. We wouldn't cast out a baby, a china dish or a family heirloom. Yet we are instructed to cast our "cares" on Him. Whatever you are caring about, cast it on the Lord!

The word used for care is better translated "solicitudes." Solicitudes are those things that we are anxious or concerned

about. In contrast, our Father uses the word *epirhippto* for casting. Literally, it means "to throw upon"! That's right, "throw," as if the care were of no value at all. Have no regard for it. Dismiss it totally.

Why does God ask us to be so radical about our solicitudes? Because "he careth for you"! That's right. While you are caring for it, He is caring for you. He loves you too much to see you twisted with pain because of something that you shouldn't even be carrying.

God has no problem making the thing leave you alone. The struggle is getting you to loose your grip on it. So He speaks to you, not to the thing bothering you. He speaks directly to you and says, "Throw it down!"

Can you do it? You must. If not, it will continue to live off of your strength, sucking up your joy like the hungry mouth of a nursing child. Now can you see what God is saying? You are nursing your enemy, giving strength to your own emotional nightmare. In the name of Jesus, throw it down!

"He careth" is the final point of this scriptural argument against stress. Peter says, "for he careth for you." The word *careth* represents a perpetual, continual, ongoing attitude of God. It literally means He is "concerned" or "interested" in you. That sounds weak until you realize that you are His only interest and His major concern. While you have esteemed all things around you, God is very focused in His interest. He says, Throw down the thing that has become a solicitude in your life, because I esteem nothing above My interest in you! Please release that hindrance before its greedy sucking depletes you, God's daughter, and leaves you empty, void and in a state of despair!

Dear daughters, as we embark upon new horizons and discuss other issues, I want to explain why I am challenging you to neuter the things that would limit you. To neuter is to leave the issue impotent. It may still exist, but it is

powerless to reproduce in your life. A lady once asked me, "How do I forget my past?" I knew that she was really saying, I can't help but remember what happened to me. I responded, "Forgetting your past doesn't mean you develop selective amnesia. You may still remember the events, but the pain of them has been removed like a stinger from a bee. The bee still buzzes, but he is not a threat because his sting is gone." No one is afraid of being raped by a neutered man. His threat is destroyed. That's what God wants to do to your doubts and fears. He wants them rendered impotent, void of passion and listlessly lying around in your mind as facts with no power over you.

There will be no offspring or side effects of these traumatic events, because you have neutered them. They are gone from you like ashes poured from an urn. They are tossed into the tempestuous sea of forgetfulness. It is finished! These are the powerful words Jesus exclaimed from the cross. Having said these words, He soon died to the things that were tormenting Him. The nails continued to exist, as did the cross, but their power over Him was destroyed. He had moved into another realm. So should you, my daughter. When life seems unfair and uncertain, do not be denied and do not be delayed by nurturing things that should be neutered. Just throw them on your stack of learning experiences and keep moving on.

What is the moral of these wise words? Here it is, short and sweet. If you can nurture negatives through the milk of your will, then you can nurture positives. You can raise a business up and keep it going against all odds with your tenacious, relentless spirit. If you can nurture a fear, you can nurture a child through a crisis, a husband through an illness or a part-time job into an executive position. You are strong in your spirit. You are full of milk. Whatever you touch need not depart, because you have what it takes to succeed. I only caution you to refrain from nurturing

things that are destructive. You will need wisdom to choose. Know your own strength. You have marveled at my strength as a man of God. To know my strength will not always help you. If you are going to cope with life, you must know your own. Do you have weaknesses? Sure, we all do. But the greatest of all weaknesses is the inability to recognize and capitalize on your own strength and self-reliance.

Do you mind if I pray with you as a good father always should? Let us pray these words together, just you and I.

Father,

Help us to realize that we often contribute to our own storms. We keep alive things that should be released, and we release many things that You wanted us to keep alive. We repent for our lack of trust and faith and, more importantly, we make a commitment to capitalize on these times and experiences that have caused so much pain. Oh, dear Lord, we thank You for letting us be alive to whisper this humble prayer. There is no doubt that if You had not watched over us, we would not be here. So thank You, Father, for giving each of us another chance. Armed with these experiences and Your presence, I am sure I will be fine. In Jesus' name. Amen.

Chapter Nine

Why Women War
Against Each Other

$\mathcal{I}$f you think about it a moment, you will recognize that this statement is true: Women war against each other. Here are three strong reasons why.

1. Isolation Syndrome

I remember playing in the yard with my friends. Being country boys, we played very primitive games. We were not exposed to expensive, exotic hobbies. Our games were simplistic and rather communal. They required interaction

and teamwork. We shared victories and defeats. We strategized how to defeat the other team. We shared secrets, and we planned in huddles how we were going to overcome the defenses of the other team.

Rarely do you find boys trained in isolation. They generally have the kinds of toys that require competitiveness. While this later creates some negatives as it relates to male stress and competitiveness, still it teaches many positives as it relates to learning how to interact with members of the same sex. Genuine interest in the opposite sex comes later.

Our first fascination was with frogs and the little boys who caught them. We thought girls were silly as they shrieked and ran away from a toad or some other animal we were trying to capture and hold hostage! I know this may sound a little antiquated compared to the children of today whose entertainment must be bought in a box and plugged into a circuit. But such were the times in which I was reared.

Anyway, through watching football we learned admiration and respect for the performance of other men. Even today most men are performance-oriented.

Some of the struggles little girls faced came from being raised playing with dolls that became trusted confidantes. But dolls can't speak. They always agree, and they never divulge secrets. Girls were not raised playing communal games that required planning, sharing and interaction.

Even the games that brought girls together were not team sports. Jump rope, hopscotch and other games required little working together and planning. A favorite of little girls of the time were toy kitchens and tea sets. They were playing house and planning marriage. Little girls were rehearsing family styles while we boys were jumping off rocks with toy guns. No wonder women are so relational in terms of male and female relationships. The poor guy doesn't know what hit him when he stands at the altar and tries to get his

lips to say, "I do." He doesn't know what it means, but she has been practicing this home life thing since she was four years old. She has been playing mommy all of her life, but little boys never played daddy! Sadly, now many of us do not know how to play!

Obviously, problems arise when the rehearsed woman comes together with the unrehearsed man. But there is another challenging area beyond the marital relationship. The little girl has spent her life playing games that brought her into a family setting with her children, her husband and her house! But what happens when she has to work with other women who do not fit into her frame of reference?

I'll tell you what happens: There is an extreme distrust. Strange conflicts break out over territory and space. Sadly, we are not teaching our little girls how to work in a world that is more densely populated with women than with men. By the time they are in junior high and exposed to other girls in the chess club or on the girls' basketball team, they have already left the formative years. They are well formed, even precocious, in their opposite-sex skills. They are so mature in that area that they know what they want out of those relationships while the young man is discovering the animalistic, primal call of the jungle mating routine. His prey is more advanced, and he ends up captured by the game!

Her area of vulnerability is centered around her struggle to find a place in her territory for other females. They were not in the original blueprint, and now here they come all dressed up and in the way! "She thinks she's cute!" they grumble. In reality, they think she's cute; that is the whole problem. There is a great need for women to respect each other. I realize many men need to be instructed in how to respect women. Might I point out that you cannot teach men to respect women if these men are reared by women who don't respect other women. I speak of men reared by

women because, I'm sad to say, fewer and fewer men are being reared by men at all in today's culture.

Hence there are real struggles when we later find out there is a need to develop strong female relationships and mutual respect, but there is little respect or willingness to share. Not learning to share creates problems when you are placed in an office, church or some other fish tank where you share copiers, choir robes or the attention of the minister. Intense struggles arise over territory. You will hear statements like, "This is my job!" "He told me to do that!" "What is she doing stealing my customers?" There is a fear and a distrust that doesn't come from being feminine as much as it arises from not having learned the elasticity that comes from being part of a team!

God has called you to serve in a church. It is a place where He wants to realign you and teach you relational skills. Together the women came down to the tomb to minister to the body of Christ. This is the meeting ground for women who may not have had anything in common. It is here that God teaches women how to love despite their fears and inhibitions and experience real sisterhood. I realize that many ministries are not experiencing the kind of covenant that ministers to the isolation syndrome. But there are some who are.

What causes some to experience victory and not others? Is it the teaching? Not totally, because I have been involved in great ministries that are not experiencing healing as it relates to the isolation syndrome. Their members are all scholars of the Word. Many of the members are adept in the Scriptures. They teach all the right concepts and they know all the proper techniques, but when real love goes on trial, they fail to overcome the childhood isolation that enslaves their hearts.

Neither is the isolation syndrome absent from those sanctimonious ones who fast, pray and dress like nuns,

keeping themselves, as they would say, "unspotted from the world." They often look holy and pious, bragging about their deep spiritual roots, but upon closer inspection there is a lack of love.

I have been behind the scenes of great ministries whose upper echelon sow thousands upon thousands of dollars into foreign missions but will not worship with the person across the street. It is here that the ladies' prayer group can become a discreet place to gossip under the guise of prayer. The intercessors spend more time discussing the issues with each other than they do discussing them with God. All these actions are impotent if they are not accompanied by a changed and challenged heart.

I know you are wondering, Where is healing for the isolation syndrome? It is not in the pews. It is in the hearts of those who sit in the pews. It is happening in the hearts and homes of those persons who refuse to be dragged down into a pit of paranoia and cynicism.

They have made a commitment to risk involvement and remove the layers they have built up to insulate themselves from pain. They are learning how to get involved and love one another. It was the women who prepared the body of Jesus for burial. Their incense and myrrh were meant to preserve it. I wonder what would happen to the unity and harmony of the ministry if women across the world would meet at the body of Christ and anoint Him together, sister to sister!

2. Maternal Maladies and Mistreatments

This is a second reason women war against each other. I have already confessed that my wife says I treat my girls differently from my sons. I love them equally but differently. Maybe it is because of how enamored I am by my girls' fragile fragrance of budding femininity. Whatever the contributing factor, there is no difference in my quality of

love, but I confess there may be a little difference in my expression of that love. I may seem a little harder on the boys because I know full well what they will have to face as men in this cold, coarse world. But if I am guilty of sweetening the pot when it comes to my ruffle-clad Easter lilies, then my wife is also guilty of letting my sons get away with murder!

Isn't it strange that when the children want an easy yes, they know which parent to ask? My little girls will walk right past their mother and ask me if they can have this or that. My boys, on the other hand, always ask their mother first. Her naïveté plays right into their hand, as she has no idea what it's like to be a boy! She will often overcompensate by being a pushover for their needs. All right, I admit it. We are both guilty! I cater to the girls and train the boys while she caters to the boys and trains the girls. But that's fine as long as both parents are there to balance the training aspect against the catering aspect. Through both parents the children are both catered to and trained well!

The problem comes when one parent is absent or does not contribute to the nurturing process of the children. What happens when the girl is raised by a woman who doesn't realize that her daughter must get Daddy's love and Mother's training from the same source? This can throw the whole equilibrium of childhood out of sync. It is especially detrimental when the mother is dictatorial with the daughter but permissive and accommodating with the son. What kind of message would that send to the daughter about who is important in that house?

If mother always fixes breakfast for her son and tells her daughter of similar age to get up and fix her own, is she subconsciously telling her daughter that men are to be favored and girls are not important? I am not referring to conscious abuse, although that too happens in many cases. Sometimes when an abused woman rears a daughter she

tries too hard to prepare her against the cold, bitter winds of the only life she has known. She may inadvertently wound the child she is trying to reinforce by not balancing discipline with affection.

Unfortunately, many daughters were reared by mothers who were unduly critical. These mothers, who probably meant only good, were attempting to train, but their methods were so harsh that they became professional critics. They murmured praise only when their daughters succeeded, but they screamed insults when they failed. They wanted to prepare them, but instead they impaired them. I bleed for these little girls who have been planted full of the seed of self-loathing. They have borne the blame in their hearts for failed marriages and broken homes. Deep down inside they feel that everything is their fault.

It is terrible to live under the harsh words of a bitter critic. Many have been beaten down with cords, fists and even scriptures. They have cried themselves to sleep. They have wished for death at early ages. They have known the harsh hopelessness of being trapped in a house with a strong dictatorial attitude. This situation transcends cultures and economics. We need only look back a few years to a motion picture called *Mommy Dearest* that riveted the nation with a picture of what can exist even behind the marbled walls and strong pillars of the rich and famous. It happened there, and it can happen in the ghetto apartments of angry mothers whose hopelessness turns to rage against the only persons who are left in the house. That girl reminds Mother of herself. Mother fears that the girl might end up in the same condition she is in, so Mother has a tantrum and the daughter is locked in a nightmare.

Whether the attitude expresses itself in the extremes I have just described or just in a slight trace of bias, it is a legitimate area of concern. Many mothers have double standards when it comes to what they expect from their

daughters versus what they require of their sons. This problem is amplified when Dad doesn't balance out man's instincts to be fascinated by opposites.

I realize that there are many mother-daughter relationships that are whole, healthy and vibrant, and I applaud them. My concern is never with those who are whole. It is with the fragmented. I am always excited to see those who have achieved success. They are the testimonies that strengthen the emotionally impoverished with the faith they need to know it can be done.

> And Jesus answering said unto them, They that are whole need not a physician; but they that are sick (Luke 5:31, KJV).

Understand that real ministry comes to the needy. If what I'm saying is not a prescription you need right now, take it anyway. It might serve as an ounce of prevention against future attacks or at least equip you to help the hurting you will encounter as you minister to those around you. This is not an accusation or an indictment against all women, but some have fallen into these traps and have thereby undermined their daughters' morale. Please don't be one of them!

Many women today have found themselves in a state of single parenting. They did not request it, and they do not prefer it, but for whatever reason it became a reality in their lives. God is giving them the grace to survive. He is helping them and assisting them as only He can. They are women who through desertion, death or the tragedy of divorce have been left with the task of parenting.

Please, please hear me. Today many other women are choosing of their own accord to be mothers without fathers. They are deciding to have children without husbands; it is becoming fashionable to have non-traditional families. I ask them, How dare you decide to raise a child with a void that could have been prevented?

DADDY LOVES HIS GIRLS

It is arrogant for you to think you are so perfect that you can rear a child and give him or her both aspects of parenting. You may be a wonderful, successful, intelligent woman. You might be the bionic mother. But you are still not a father. Whether this society wants to admit it or not, God gave children for marriage. The man and the woman were jointly challenged to be fruitful. It takes both to procreate, and it works best when both contribute to the development of that fruit. Don't rob your children of a wonderful level of wholeness.

A father's love is essential to good healthy development. I know you can do it alone. But there are going to be some challenges you face in bringing balance — too many challenges for you to choose this plight for yourself. But if for some reason you are left to bring the children up alone, God is able! You can do it but not without the assistance of your heavenly Father, whose wisdom will become a resource center for help and guidance along the way!

If you are not a Christian, stop and give your life to Jesus before you allow your pain to pollute the way you influence your children. If you have been the victim of any of the abuses detailed in this discourse, or even if your struggles as a child were slight injustices that caused secret pains, I want to recommend the Father who will never leave you nor forsake you. No one can keep you from His favors. He is waiting to give you what you missed. His blood can heal the breach!

3. Gender Oppression: Deeply Embedded, Seldom Defined

This is a third reason women war against each other. Many women in this country have been abused and poorly treated. Anytime we have been oppressed it creates a certain sense of lowliness. This world in which we live is excellent at saying to various groups, Stay in your place. We

imprison people with stereotypes and punish them if they escape the typecast role we have determined for them.

Years ago the dominant trend of thought in this nation was a concept that suggested the woman's place was in the kitchen. She was treated like a second-class citizen. She was denied the right to vote. Amazingly, the terrible racism that exists in this country and many others is rivaled only by sexism, which also stands at attention and salutes the flag. How tragic that we have allowed the color and shape of the container to distort our perception of its contents.

Some time ago I was interviewed by an intelligent, vibrant, female religious news reporter who wanted to do an article on me for the paper. After years of investing, saving and struggling through financial challenges, my wife and I had finally reached a place where we could afford our dream house. We were shocked to realize that not everyone shared our enthusiasm. We found ourselves having to defend our right to life, liberty and the pursuit of happiness.

You see, this small, Southern town newspaper thought it inappropriate for a man of God to have a nice home or to be successful in business. They sent a reporter out to further ridicule us for purchasing our home. Well, I began the interview by attempting to explain that I have preached the gospel like Paul from all economic levels. I have been abased and abounded. I have slept in shanties and preached in garages.

It was years before I did any abounding and experienced some of the amenities of the better side of town. But now I have slept in penthouse suites and eaten caviar. I am a living testimony that God will answer prayers. In spite of all of that, the message is still the same. Jesus saves!

I know both how to be abased, and I know how
to abound: every where and in all things I am

instructed both to be full and to be hungry, both
to abound and to suffer need (Phil. 4:12, KJV).

Anyway, I attempted to explain that I am both a businessman and a minister. God has bountifully blessed both of
these areas. But I also wanted her to understand that there
had been times in preaching when I couldn't get together
gas money to get back home. God sovereignly blessed me
to make the kind of business decisions that brought some
semblance of security to my family. Why is that a disgrace
in the secular community and even among under-informed
Christians?

I did not realize that any form of success offends people
who are at a different stage in their lives, particularly when
they define piety as poverty. It is permissible for football
players and baseball players to be wealthy. It is permissible
for entertainers and dancers to be wealthy while parading
across the stage in scant apparel. We have no qualms with
those who entertain us being blessed through their giftings:
the dentist who cleans and caps our teeth, the actress, the
rapper whose lyrics encourage violence, sin and so on.

We even accept motivational speakers prospering, as long
as it is not the man or woman God has chosen to feed our
souls, bury our dead and prepare our hearts for eternity.

When the reporter suggested that ministers should not
live as well as other professionals, I realized that a spirit
of oppression was at work in the mentality of some people in that city and many others throughout our country.
She reasoned that Jesus was poor and would not be
pleased with those who serve Him having any of these
advantages.

In reply, I pointed out that Jesus wasn't poor. If He were,
He would not have been able to maintain Luke, a physician
who left his practice; Matthew, a tax collector; or Peter, a
businessman, and put them on staff full-time for three

years. They must have been on some sort of payroll. They were men with families!

> But if any provide not for his own, and specially for those of his own house, he hath denied the faith, and is worse than an infidel (1 Tim. 5:8, KJV).

Jesus had a treasurer (John 12:4-6; 13:29). You don't need a treasurer if you have no money! He had taxes to pay (Matt. 17:24-27). Although He was a carpenter's son, I never read where He spent His precious time building houses. We needed His words more than we needed His building. In fact, as early as age twelve, He began to let His family know that His business was His Father's business.

> And he said unto them, How is it that ye sought me? wist ye not that I must be about my Father's business? (Luke 2:49, KJV).

Even when He was being taken from judgment hall to judgment hall, He did not look like a beggar. While He was dying on the cross, His wardrobe was the envy of the worldly men who crucified Him. His coat was so nice that those poorly paid Roman soldiers were gambling at the foot of the cross trying to get that "seamless robe."

> Then the soldiers, when they had crucified Jesus, took his garments, and made four parts, to every soldier a part; and also his coat: now the coat was without seam, woven from the top throughout. They said therefore among themselves, Let us not rend it, but cast lots for it, whose it shall be: that the scripture might be fulfilled, which saith, They parted my raiment among them, and for my vesture they did cast lots. These things therefore the soldiers did (John 19:23-24, KJV).

Finally, I said to the reporter, "It was only a few years ago that the media would be interviewing you as a woman because you shouldn't be a reporter. They would say that you should be at home making biscuits." She admitted this was true. She had faced abuse and mistreatment by being a pioneer in her profession. I am glad I live in a country that does not require I live my life in alignment with the trends of those around me. Aren't you?

What does that have to do with women? I am glad you asked. It is discrimination anytime you say a person should not have this because they are that — whether the "that" is their race, their occupation or even their gender. For ministers, there is tremendous occupational discrimination in this country. It is a societal oppression trying to force its bigotry and intolerance on others, and it must be renounced!

We have the right to climb mountains and stretch the wings God has given us, our sons and daughters! Discrimination causes disloyalties and jealousies even among ministers. Oppression creates disgruntled victims who turn against each other because they are put in a negative light. They begin to blame one another. In the same way, sexism has left even the women who have been victims of it bickering among themselves. Satan's tactics are still the same: divide and conquer. He is after women in the same fashion.

The Bible says that there is an enmity between the woman and the serpent (Satan) (Gen. 3:15). There always has been and there always will be. But, thank God, many ministries are fighting for all oppressed people to rise and be healed. I have been a longtime supporter of women in this nation and in the body of Christ. Christ was an obvious emancipator of oppressed women, from the woman taken in adultery to the woman at the well. He was always liberating them and upgrading their standard of living.

Without realizing the severity of it, many women have been dealing with the trauma and the struggle of oppression. There are many side effects that influence how they see each other. This same woman who interviewed me for the newspaper had forgotten just that quickly her own plight and struggle. How can we attack people for doing what we are trying to do?

> And Jesus knew their thoughts, and said unto them, Every kingdom divided against itself is brought to desolation; and every city or house divided against itself shall not stand (Matt. 12:25, KJV).

The enemy's strength exists when he can break the unity of the oppressed. He doesn't want us to unite against all forms of oppression and discrimination. It is all criminal, and there are no acceptable forms of oppressing any people for any reason! Many women do not recognize the damage that years of oppression will do to their confidence and self-esteem. It is time for us to discuss and define oppression in all of its forms. Its strength lies in its ability to hide and its ability to divide. Let us not allow it to hide as it takes on various forms, and for God's sake we cannot allow it to separate any of us who have fallen prey to its vicious grip!

The reporter and I parted with a deeper respect one for the other, because both of our lives had been attacked by those who would say to us, Stay in your place and keep quiet! Today everyone has at one time or another been the victim of some sort of discrimination. Perhaps in some way we can better understand the plight of others when we have experienced it ourselves. My experience had come from being a black man but more recently from being a Christian minister. Hers had come although she was white — in a small rural region where the population is less than one hundred thousand and five percent black

— because she was a woman who dared to get out of her place. Regardless of the reason for the attack, the fence was just as high and the dogs barked just as loudly, saying, Do not cross the line, or we will attack you!

Remember, oppression in any form is oppression; it is a painful pill that has been crammed in the mouth of many. Women of all colors have had to endure it in silence. They will stand beside all those who have been oppressed. But the problem is difficult, because gender abuse is not discussed, and there are some side effects of it that need to be underlined.

In some strange way, oppression can create self-loathing. It tears down loyalty. If I never see anyone who looks like me in certain settings, I subconsciously begin to think that there is something wrong with those who are like me! Any oppressed people begin to bicker among themselves and complain. They begin to blame one another and argue. If you hold people hostage they begin to devour each other. It is perhaps the hopelessness of feeling trapped.

Many women who are creative, assertive and aggressive have had to smother that aggressiveness to fit in certain circles. When a woman does spread her wings in the sun, she is often snubbed not only by men but also by other women. You would expect to find these prejudices among men, but even some women still find it difficult to work for another woman. What a statement — to aspire to a position of leadership, while preferring not to submit to anyone of your own gender who is in the position. It is a sign that oppression has affected your image of yourself, your race or your gender. How can I not respect someone of my own gender, race or occupation for achieving in an area that I aspire to attain?

The tragedy cuts deep into our inner hearts. We cannot get others to purge the innocent bloodshed of captives locked up behind small-mindedness if we ourselves have

not exorcised the demons of discontentment that allow us to reject our own.

People who have been oppressed have a tendency to operate like crabs trying to escape from a barrel. Each one is trying to get up. When he sees another crab trying to do what he wants to do, he pulls him down. This crab-like mentality is a common characteristic of those who have been oppressed. It graphically depicts an ambiguous lack of self-esteem. It creates a peer pressure that says you are acceptable as long as you stay on certain levels, but if you reach for your freedom we will pull you down.

That is too high for a woman (preacher, Mexican, etc.) to go. As painful as it is to be criticized, I challenge you not to allow others to pull you back. If God has given you the grace to go forth, do it. If no one had ever challenged public opinion, we would still be driving in a horse and buggy, blacks would be riding the back of the bus and women of all colors would be stuck on the front porch sipping iced tea and exchanging recipes instead of working in corporate America.

Life is too long to spend it bent down to keep from standing out. And it is too short to wait on people to change their minds before you plunge ahead with your giftings! In the interest of time, you must urgently pursue what God has given you the grace to attain and then let your critics adjust to you. I feel like God is about to loose some precious woman who has been struggling with public opinion versus personal ambitions. I would say to you right now, there is greatness in you that is waiting to be unleashed, and in the name of Jesus, woman, thou art loosed!

> Shake thyself from the dust; arise, and sit down, O Jerusalem: loose thyself from the bands of thy neck, O captive daughter of Zion (Is. 52:2, KJV).

115

It is healthy for all of us to see liberation. It is not at the expense of men that women are released — not if it is done God's way. When a woman is freed from oppression, she becomes more satisfied and more of a partner to her companion rather than an accessory in his life. Many women find fulfillment mothering their children, and that is certainly a wonderful calling. I believe motherhood is a call of God and not just a biological conglomeration of fluids. We need mothers to prepare the next generation. There are other women who prefer to contribute to this world on other levels. They should not have to be ridiculed in the workplace, frustrated at the family reunion and ostracized at the ladies' club because they chose a different path.

The change comes when you as a woman respect yourself and other women around you. Even men need to see women respecting each other. It sets a precedent of value and instructs us as to your own inner worth. Boys need to hear their mother speaking well of other women. Daughters need to hear it. We impact other people with subtle signals. When they hear you speaking highly of people they will become positive and motivated to speak highly of others also. Cynical people always reproduce after their own kind.

Oppression's greatest victim is the person who falls prey to the opinion of those who hold you captive. By falling prey I mean allowing their opinion to influence how you see yourself. That is too much power to give anybody. Stop crouching down and stand up. If you don't, you will begin to agree with those who oppress you. They cannot hold you down. But you can hold yourself down. They may delay you, but they cannot deny your ability. You are truly imprisoned by your own attitude. Your only limit is the lock you place on your own creativity.

Now to the heart of the matter. Jesus said, "Love your

neighbor as yourself" (Matt. 19:19, NAS). If you really want to know how you feel about yourself, you may evaluate that anytime you want by looking at how you treat others like you! If that test reveals that you have a struggle with self-loathing, ask the Lord to heal you. You will know you are healed when you respect those around you who are similar to you! Respect means respecting each other in the workplace as well as in the worship place.

If you respect her, you will not try to belittle her or overstep proper boundaries in how you treat her husband. How can you say you respect women and step over them trying to attract the attention of their husbands? I am amazed as we travel how many women will walk over top of my wife to speak to me. They never even acknowledge her. You can never honor me by dishonoring the one with whom I have shared all things. How disrespectful. A man who stepped over me to hug my wife might be jeopardizing his longevity on the earth, and yet women do that all the time without the slightest regard for me or my wife.

If I asked them, Do you respect women?, they would say yes. But the answer is really no! They give no respect because they have none to give. Or worse still is the compulsive flirt whose spirit of rivalry needs to be fed by flirting with other women's husbands. She is not just lonely. She is so full of low self-esteem that she creates these contests to inflate a sagging ego with some evidence of worth. There are some women who didn't have any interest in your husband until you married him. Now they are delirious with desire. Please. As my children would say, Give me a break!

Respecting each other is reflected in how you honor marriage. How can you say you respect her and then flirt with her spouse? Respect means "to honor and esteem as valuable." This attitude starting in our churches would usher in real healing for women who have had trouble

trusting even close friends and relationships. This could start a tremendous wave of healing. But it starts in the heart of one woman who says, I refuse to assassinate the character, rights and lifestyle of my sister. I treat her as if she is me and I am her. I will never get up by pulling her down. I will break the curse of the oppressed and thereby destroy the cancer that is eating away at the heart of many women.

You and I have examined just a few contributions to the demise of female relationships. The list is incomplete, but we have touched on jealousies and mother-daughter relationships. I don't think the list of problems is as important as the list of answers. What can you do to bridge the gulf between you and other women? How can you invest in the self-esteem of your sisters? What affirmation can you give that would be beneficial to the hurting woman?

Look way down into your heart beyond your pains and rejections — beyond the habits they have created for how you treat other women. You have to rummage through the recreated heart that the Holy Spirit places within you and allow God to use you as a paramedic of mercy. You have to change the world one person at a time.

If you have a daughter that you have been critical of, start with her. What does it matter who is right and who is wrong if you lose the child? Even if you have to call across the country, call her. Explain why you haven't always been as supportive as you wanted to be. Tell her about your own pain. Tell her she deserves to know why the rage has been acted out on her. Apologize to her and tell her you want to see the relationship healed. It may not change all at once. It takes more than a U-turn to make up for the distance and the time you travel in the wrong direction on the highway. But it is a step in the right direction. If you just stay on course, you will get to where you ought to be in time.

Maybe it's your mother or your sister with whom you have been at odds.* Perhaps it has chipped away at what should have been a strong relationship. Today in Jesus' name take the initiative and begin to correct the damage. Don't be childish and argue about "who hit whom first." You are bigger than that. God is dealing with your heart, and you should move toward healing. You have been asking God to restore things you had lost. Well, this is part of it.

Make things right. Do not blame anyone. Just allow the Holy Spirit to work. Your flesh will scream, fear of rejection will come, but many of you have nothing to lose. Your relationship is in a terminal condition anyway. The whole communication between you and her has only survived on life-support systems. You cannot worship through this. God wants to heal your heart.

It is my prayer that you would allow the light to shine brightly upon you as a channel of expression for someone who needs encouragement. It is a habit well worth forming. If you give it out, it will come back to you — pressed down, shaken together and running over will [women] give unto your bosom (Luke 6:38)!

---

*My daughters, I didn't allow you to fight when you were small. Do not allow life to later turn you into crooked-nosed, hateful, cynical women who always have something negative to say about one another. You are sisters. You are entitled by your father's blood. God bless you. I am praying for you!

Chapter Ten

Sometimes He Must Say No

$\mathcal{O}$ne of the greatest challenges to our faith are those moments when we must endure the cold blight of a disappointment. The greater the anticipation, the greater the disappointment when we fail to receive what we have anticipated.

Much has been written about the blessings and fulfillment of God's promises, and rightfully so. But as a father I thought I would be remiss not to prepare you for those occasions when life doesn't turn out like you would expect.

I know firsthand the sinking feeling of dejection that comes into your heart when things fall through. It feels almost as though an earthquake has struck in your heart. The very things you were counting on and standing on have slipped from under you, and something within begins to sink. The floor gives way, and everything you have planned seems meaningless. The temptation is to have an all-out pity party complete with candles, cake and ice cream!

There is no shield that can keep away the days that come to teach our hearts submission to God's will and purpose for us. There are no cards that are so poetic, no roses that are so fragrant that they dismiss for us the tingling sensations of brokenness that come upon us when we see our expectations cave in. We take those expectations and mold them into a strange caricature of a person we wish we had to hold. It's a feeling that will bring the most mature into a fetal position. It comes as if it will not leave, but you can be sure that is not so. It will go, and the sun will come again and rebuke the clouds that have hidden the light of God's purpose from shining through to you.

Words seem empty and caresses seem sterile, almost as if those who embrace us have wrapped their emotions in a glove. Their touch seems impersonal and ineffective — as if they are insulated from the real pain we feel. Perhaps it is not they who are detached and insulated. Perhaps it is our grieving heart and broken spirit that have isolated us from the warmth of their expressions. We are there and not there, preoccupied with the cold blight of the moment.

I know you probably don't need these rather morbid-sounding words today. But save these words and bind them up, for each of us will see days when comfort becomes comforting. You are no exception. It is my desire as a father to prepare you as best I can for the days when you have invested much effort and perhaps even much prayer into

121

things that fail to come to fruition. These are the days that weaken the pulse and send the bitter taste of bile to our taste buds. We live on, we swallow; but there is the bitter reminder that lingers within, leaving us feeling like failures.

As much as it pleases Him to bless you, there will be moments when everything you try goes up in smoke. There will be moments when the one you counted on most walks away and leaves you groping through blinding tears and wailing questions of why. You will not need these words today. But someday when rejection comes and leaves you feeling worthless, find these words and dust them off. They will keep. You see, my daughters, truth is timeless and age-less. It will always be there, undaunted and unchanged — as fresh as it was when you first perceived it.

There is the strangest association that attaches itself to youth. It is the feeling of being invincible and untouchable. There is a myth that exists in the hearts of some young people that makes them think they are exempt from the brokenness of life. I think pain is more painful when it is unexpected. So pain comes as a shock to the young and even to some Christians who live under the illusion that they cannot experience the sharp, stabbing pains of disappointment. Yet life affords all of its participants an equal opportunity to experience pain.

Deeply etched within the faces of the aged is the reality that life often goes awry. Beneath the wisp of wintry hair and weathered eyes is a knowing that danger is always closer and more tempestuous than they would have thought in their youth. The constant nagging of the aged is birthed from the valley of their own experiences and perils. They buzz like an alarm in your ears. It becomes an irritant to youthful ears that have no time or interest in caution. Yet hearken and take note: There are some encounters that can take the wind out of your sails, the curls out of your hair and the gleam out of your smile.

Perhaps the greatest difference between the young and the elderly is not the stiffened joints and aged muscles. Perhaps it is not the dimly lit eyes or the trembling of feeble wrists. Perhaps it is the reality that burns like embers behind their graying crowns. It is the places where they have walked. It is the reality that plans and goals can be circumvented by the most disappointing of times, leaving you learning the art of patience and the acceptance of a denied request.

Nevertheless, there is within the human capacity a tenacious instinct of survival that kicks in when we are at our lowest. It enables us to succeed through the storms of life. They will come, but they will not overthrow you if you learn to trust God even when you can't trace Him. You may not know why you have had to face the chilling winds of despair, but trust God to renew you. Just live on.

He is so wise. He knows the greater truths that can only be realized by eyes that can behold today and tomorrow in one glance. His vision supersedes our nearsighted requests centered around the thirst of the day and not the droughts of the future. He must, as a good Father, deny requests that would insult the greater destiny He has prepared for those who are His. He is a God of tough love. He has the ability to firmly decline a request when you would be endangered by a positive response. In short, He loves you enough to say no!

Submission is the word buzzing in my brain. I know it is the word that many feminine hearts resist even when they read it in the Word. But submission can be a friend to the struggling heart of a victim that has been chained to the will of God. Rather than burn your hands and hearts wrestling to break free from the grip that holds you for your own protection, just submit. Why would you resist the One to whom you have entrusted your future? It is safe to trust Him. He will not fail you. He is the Bishop of your soul!

For ye were as sheep going astray; but are now
returned unto the Shepherd and Bishop of your
souls (1 Pet. 2:25, KJV).

Who is the bishop of your soul? Is he a portly, kind gen-
tleman walking around a sanctuary in robes, reciting
prayers? No. That is an ecclesiastical definition of a man
who has churches under his charge. He is like a general in
the ecclesiastical order of various denominations; others
prefer the term superintendent or president. But this is not
an ecclesiastical definition. It is a theological one, and it
refers also to oversight — not the oversight of churches but
the oversight of souls!

In short, He is the overseer, the protector. He watches out
for you like a lifeguard at a pool. Imagine that a lifeguard,
seated upon his perch far above swimmers — whose only
interest was in the thrills and chills of play — sees someone
about to be engulfed by impending danger. Because he
cares, he leaps from his perch and dives into the very
waters where he sensed danger. He makes swift strokes
toward the victim, whose next move will send her into the
abyss of true destruction.

Just before the cold grasp of disaster devours its victim,
the lifeguard swoops her out of danger. Did he interrupt the
continuity of the festivities? Yes, he did. Did he perhaps
bruise a rib while rescuing her? Perhaps. She may even be
embarrassed and humiliated. But the real truth of the matter
is that he saw something she didn't see and rescued her.

This is the kind of bishop you have. He watches out for
you, and His eyes are keen! When He says no, you ought
to say yes! He would never interrupt you or embarrass you
before your friends if He didn't see something ahead that
necessitated the answer He gave. You ought to praise Him
right now — on the beach, ribs bruised, head spinning, out
of breath, people staring, but alive!

The real issue is a matter of trust — trusting the Father to know what is best for any of us. Dear daughters, hear me well. I've told you before and I'll tell you again: He will not withhold any good thing from you. If it were good, He would have said yes. That thing that is not coming to you may seem good. But either the timing is wrong, or from His position He can see that the future of it is bleak. I have always believed that people who only thank God for delivering them from what happened are just scraping the surface of praise. The real praise comes when you start thanking Him for what could have happened but didn't, because of His swift grace!

Celebration should be leaping out of your heart. Trusting God transforms calamity into testimony. Knowing He cares too much for you to abuse you and He is too wise to be wrong causes a wounded heart to serenade the heavens. When we begin to know Him rather than just serve Him, we can trust His vision, His wisdom and His insight. He can no more make an explanation to you before He snatches you out of the water than a lifeguard can teach a class in the middle of the sea while a victim is about to drown. You must trust Him when He does not explain what you thought you needed to know.

The closed door is a blessing. Many people rejoice about the opening of doors. I guess that is a blessing, especially if you needed the door open and only God could do it. I can understand why the heart sings when the hand of God moves the obstacle out of the way. The eye can see the way made, and the feet begin to dance toward a brighter future. That is not beyond my understanding.

But I want to challenge you to go a step further into the deeper sovereign truth of a closed door. We can readily accept His authority when it is used to perform what we know to be a favor. The real challenge of submission is to submit when the human will would have chosen another

way. This is the graduation exercise of faith and the commencement service of a trust for those whose dependency and reliance is upon the manifold wisdom of God.

These things saith he that is holy, he that is true, he that hath the key of David, he that openeth, and no man shutteth; and shutteth, and no man openeth (Rev. 3:7, KJV).

Here God alludes to the power of the shut door. It is significant to understand that the shut door is just as much a move of God as the open one. It is the same mighty hand, and it is the same loving heart. It is an action predetermined by the wisdom of a Father who knows what is best. He does emphatically shut doors. We have not taught enough about the shut door. The mention of the key of David implies that the door is not just shut but locked. This is amplified when he says that no man can open it. There is no purpose in any of us trying to pray open, work open or pry open what God has shut.

You know it is a shut door when it will not open. I know this guide seems vague, because many of us have had to pray to get a door open from where the enemy was trying to discourage us. This is an issue where great spirituality is a great benefit. If the door is just closed by the enemy, and he is trying to get you to give up on your dream, prayer and praise will unlock it! But if the door is closed by a sovereign decision of an all-wise God, and prayer and praise do not open it, then you must accept His decision.

That doesn't mean the door cannot be opened. It just means that "no man" can open it. If God doesn't open the door, it cannot be opened. If He doesn't do it, you don't want it to be done. By now you should know that He does what is best for you. There is a difference between a door Satan has jammed and a door God has locked from you.

It may not be a permanent lock. It may be a timed lock.

God may be saying, Not at this time. If it is a timed no, it may be God's way of bringing me to a place of submission and my flesh under control. Only a praying heart that turns to Him can determine the answer. That is a good time to hang up the telephone, cut off the television set and fall down on bended knees. Prayer does work. If you pray, He does have the key, and He can open the door!

> If I shut up the heavens so that there is no rain,
> or if I command the locust swarms to eat up all
> of your crops, or if I send an epidemic among
> you, then if my people will humble themselves
> and pray, and search for me, and turn from their
> wicked ways, I will hear them from heaven and
> forgive their sins and heal their land. I will listen,
> wide awake, to every prayer made in this place
> (2 Chr. 7:13-15, TLB).

If in prayer the hinges do not move and the latch does not unclasp, then we must conclude that God has for our betterment shut the door. If He has shut it, do not pout like a little girl who has become accustomed to getting her way. A spoiled child is an insult to a training parent. It just says that you have not accepted discipline. Perhaps that is what is happening now. The spoiled child may be getting weaned from the tantrums and sulking that accompany the untrained. This is hard, but it is also right!

I want you to learn the art of rejoicing when He says no. Rejoice when things don't go the way you planned. Rejoice, because if Satan is at work, your attitude will make his efforts futile. If you are going to praise God anyway, his efforts are counterproductive. He has no need to attack you if he is not getting the proper reaction. No one wants to attack someone who keeps smiling. The enemy will get discouraged if you don't encourage him with your depression!

But I also want you to learn the ability to thank God

when the answer is irrevocably, unalterably and emphatically no! It may sound insane, but trust me on this. It is all good! You see, He is working on your behalf — of course He is. If He says no, I want you to thank Him. Some of my greatest moments with God have come when I said yes to His corrections and decisions. Satan was defeated, and God was worshiped by my trust in His sovereign will for my life.

Doesn't that hurt? At first, but when I remind myself of God's love for me and that He would never hurt me, disappointment dissipates and love emanates from the comfort of His embrace. I am His child. I relax and say thank you.

Our problem is that we have never been loved by anyone in the way that He loves us. We have nothing with which we can compare it. His love is gentler than a mother's breast and stronger than a father's arms at the same time. It is more intimate than a lover's caress. It is more consistent than a child's affection. It is *agape*. It is God's love. If we would ever fathom it — His love alone would heal the aching of our broken heart. He absolutely adores you.

Why are you running from place to place and person to person looking for love? Have you not heard? He has been speaking to you through all of your circumstances. He is the One you need when life has wounded you and you have fallen from your nesting place like a bird. It is His hand that catches the falling soul. Then He casts it to the wind and commands it to fly again.

It is a shame that we as Christians have moved so far away from the masterful plan of salvation. We need to teach again the marvelous plan of salvation — not just the recipe of salvation, the repeat-after-me recipes that soon become canned and cold. We need to teach the chemistry of salvation. An eternal God chose you before you were ever born. His hand-picked bride, that is what you are. You *have been* selected — not *will be*. You *are* selected. You are not on trial. You are chosen.

You need to know your Father. You know so much about the church, and that is great. The church is the mother who held you in her womb and carried you with her grace. She has fed you the sincere milk from her breast. The milk of the Word has caused you to grow (1 Pet. 2:2). That is wonderful, but I am concerned because we have raised up too many children in the kingdom who know so much about their mother. They know when to worship; they know when to sit. They know all about the social order and politics. They are full of church history and programs, but they know nothing of their Father.

> For unto us a child is born, unto us a son is given: and the government shall be upon his shoulder: and his name shall be called Wonderful, Counsellor, the mighty God, the everlasting Father, the Prince of Peace (Is. 9:6, KJV).

If the church is your mother, as glorious as she is, you still need to know your Father. He is the One who produced the seed of His Word that caused you to come into being. It is His name you inherit, and your calling upon it opens up all of heaven. It is He who carries you and delivers you. If you are insecure, it is because you have spent so much time nestled near your mother's tenderness that you have not experienced your Father's strength. He is strong and mighty. He is your Father, and the devil can't stop it!

He made up His mind before you ever made that mistake. If you have repented of sin, then dismiss guilt. Guilt is the offspring of unbelief, and it insults the mercy of God. He knows your end from the beginning. Feel Him strengthening you as He is revealed inside of you. He cannot be explained. He must be revealed. Let Him be revealed in your heart right now! It is not just a man thing. It is a God thing, the creator of man. He is the epitome of masculinity. He is omnipotent, not impotent. He is the Everlasting Father.

Have ye not known? Have ye not heard? Hath it not been told you from the beginning? Have ye not understood from the foundations of the earth? It is he that sitteth upon the circle of the earth, and the inhabitants thereof are as grasshoppers; that stretcheth out the heavens as a curtain, and spreadeth them out as a tent to dwell in: That bringeth the princes to nothing; he maketh the judges of the earth as vanity. Yea, they shall not be planted; yea, they shall not be sown; yea, their stock shall not take root in the earth: and he shall also blow upon them, and they shall wither, and the whirlwind shall take them away as stubble. To whom then will ye liken me, or shall I be equal? saith the Holy One. Lift up your eyes on high, and behold who hath created these things, that bringeth out their host by number: he calleth them all by names by the greatness of his might, for that he is strong in power; not one faileth (Is. 40:21-26, KJV).

There is no need to feel left out or seek to belong to the pack. You need not seek to be a part of the gang. You have been called out and separated by God. You were not created to be popular. You were not called to cliques or clubs. You were chosen to fit in the hands of God who has already accepted you. Insecurity dissipates in the reality of divine truth. How I want you to know the height and the depth of His unfathomable love for you!

You would not be so critical of yourself or so worried about public opinion if you were to know the opinion of God. His thoughts toward you are good and not evil. He wants to dispel the myths that keep you afraid of Him. Yes, every father wants to be respected and deserves to be respected. But no good father wants his children to be

terrified of him. Neither does he want them to question his love for them. Some of you have never been secure in the love of your natural father, and it affects how you view your heavenly Father, but listen to me. There is no doubt about His love. He made the ultimate sacrifice just to prove to you the authenticity of His love.

You are so valuable that Satan held you as ransom, knowing that your Father was so rich! He asked of God, What would you give to see this woman freed? Your Father came through forty-two generations armed with love and wrapped in flesh. He said, This is how much I think she is worth. He hung His head between His shoulders and died naked on a tree because you mean so much to Him.

Never again insult His great sacrifice by questioning His love. You may not see it or understand it, but believe it. He absolutely loves you. Not just when you are right. He loves you when you are wrong. That is what gives you the power to right the wrongs you've made. He wants desperately to heal the aching heart that has believed the lies of life. You are special and vibrant, full of potential and possibilities. You are the daughter of a King. He is the King who spared no expense to pay the ransom that delivered you from the things that held you hostage. Get a clue; catch a hint; you are somebody!

These are the truths He wants every believer to know. These are the words I found in the Bible. It is a living love letter to a dying world. It is a statement of intent from a God who wants you to have it all.

His arms are outstretched. He is waiting for you in the secret place. He will not fail you. Rise up, my love, with a quickened pulse and a gleaming eye. He is all yours, and it is all good. A no from Him is as sweet as a yes. It is the evidence of His intense attraction to you and His raging love for you. Your life is about to crescendo into a symphony of praise. When His plan crescendos, you will be

glad you didn't settle for your own way. He is up to something. Do not miss it!

> Jesus saith unto them, Fill the water pots with water. And they filled them up to the brim. And he saith unto them, Draw out now, and bear unto the governor of the feast. And they bare it. When the ruler of the feast had tasted the water that was made wine, and knew not whence it was: (but the servants which drew the water knew;) the governor of the feast called the bridegroom, and saith unto him, Every man at the beginning doth set forth good wine; and when men have well drunk, then that which is worse: but thou hast kept the good wine until now (John 2:7-10, KJV).

He has saved the best for last. Do not cry if He fails to allow you to drink the common wine that others drink. We often make the mistake of comparing our situations with others'. They have received the natural wine that comes to those whose patience will not allow them to wait. The better wine comes to trusting hearts that present to Him the dismal waters of depletion and await the exhilarating jubilance of the miraculous. He has said no to what you wanted. Have you ever considered that He may be saving something far sweeter, far richer and fuller for you? He loves you.

> Dear Girls,
> I know myself I have occasionally had to disappoint your expectations. I could not always explain to you why I did what I did. It was then that I would have to endure the pained look on your face. I often denied you the right to go places where others went or do things that others did.

A good father is not a Santa Claus who gives you whatever you ask without weighing out the effects of your request. The truth be told, having a man is not having a Santa Claus. Be assured that life is not Christmas. Do not spend your life sitting in front of a cold fireplace, waiting with milk and cookies for some stranger to come. He will not be coming. I suggest that you build yourself a fire, drink your own milk and eat your own cookies.

When the Lord does send someone into your life who loves you like I do, understand that love does not mean that either of you will always get your way. It is a sharing situation with negotiations and compromises for mutual good. I know love may make an old woman feel young. It may make a balding man buy a hairpiece, but love is not immature. It is not for the frivolous. Love requires maturity, and it can require discipline and a great deal of trust.

It is my hope that the foundation of all of your relationships in life will be your relationship to your heavenly Father. Though I am but a poor caricature of His clear reality, I hope that I have in some small way reflected a little of His great love and joy toward you. I did not always say yes, and He won't say it either. But I hope when life's disappointments come, you will remember that whenever I said no it was because I wanted what was best for you so much that I was willing to see you disappointed today in order to know that you would be alive to enjoy tomorrow.

Now some ladies do not have a father to reflect upon, or he may not have even tried to be a standard by which they could perceive fatherhood.

When they face challenges, tell them about the Father's love. He cares for us. Maybe that gives purpose to our pains. We can begin to understand that out of our own experience we can speak to others who did not have the inner strength or the helpful background to withstand the pain. God wants to use you! Perhaps you can help others to trust when they are disappointed.

Can we talk? I admit I hate to see you disappointed, and I want you to always have joy. It is selfish, but I want you to like me. No one wants to be disliked, not even for a few hours. But if I sense danger in your plans, I will turn you down, even if I make you angry, because I want what is best for you. Now most of the things that we are discussing are minute issues, but these principles will help you understand when God denies you things you want, especially when it seems everyone else is getting them but you. They are significant lackings. Not every woman will be allowed to birth children. Not every woman will be a wife. Some will not be wealthy. His decisions, although varied, are not biased. He simply takes into account many variables of which we have no knowledge.

If you as my daughter can just accept that my loving you does not exempt you from correction and direction, you will bud and blossom. Just know that I am weak for you in that I would do anything for your betterment. But I am strong for you in that I will do whatever it takes to insure that I have protected you from greater dangers than temporary inconveniences and embarrassments.

As I close this letter and move on, let's take a minute for father-daughter bonding. Come a little

closer, put your hand upon my chest and feel the beating of my heart. The rhythm that you feel is steady and consistent. It has a pattern and a direction. So is my love. I want you to know what every woman needs desperately to understand and could never know without communication. I want you to know a father's heart!

Love always,
Daddy

Little lady, you are the Father's heartbeat, and He loves you so. Please do not break His heart by living in sin. He has a reason for asking you to give up areas that compromise true holiness. He isn't saying no because He is mean. He is saying no because He wants something better for you than this. He is not the kind of Father who would deny a good thing to you. If He is trying to wrench a little sin toy out of your hand, it is because He knows it will eventually destroy you, your children or your self-esteem. Let it go.

I know how hard it is to confront immorality and weakness. Many are the days I have had to crawl upon His lap and weep, asking Him to help me with myself. I know we have to be weaned from Satan's toys if we are going to be used by the Lord. But it is such a blessing when the foe is conquered, the enemy is defeated and you look beyond the test and see the joy on the other side. You will see, when you overcome, that the Father has a reward. Every time you resist temptation, whether that temptation is an extra-marital affair or the temptation to be critical and rude to others, you will see that the Father has rewards for accomplishments.

No further excuses. You know the Father is right. Off with you now. Go quickly into His presence; climb upon His knee; lay your head on His breast. Cry if you must, but talk to Him. Let Him cleanse you of sin and purge you of pride. I want you to know He loves you just as much when He says no as He does when He says yes. I will leave you with the words of one of the great hymns of the church:

> Sweet hour of prayer, sweet hour of prayer,
> That calls me from a world of care,
> And bids me, at my Father's throne,
> Make all my wants and wishes known!
> In seasons of distress and grief,
> My soul has often found relief,
> And oft escaped the tempter's snare
> By thy return, sweet hour of prayer.

Chapter Eleven

Your Father Left You Loaded!

A good man leaves his family an inheritance. I have worked feverishly to try to insure that you are left with a launching pad for your life. It may not jibe together as I have planned it, but it is my intent to leave this world with children who have been blessed with an inheritance.

A father is a provider. He should provide for more than the moment. He should provide for the future. It is foolish and ignorant not to plan for the future. I feel it is part of my duties as the head of my house to help provide security

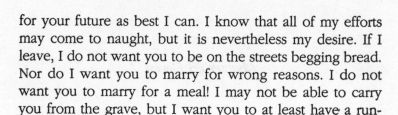

for your future as best I can. I know that all of my efforts may come to naught, but it is nevertheless my desire. If I leave, I do not want you to be on the streets begging bread. Nor do I want you to marry for wrong reasons. I do not want you to marry for a meal! I may not be able to carry you from the grave, but I want you to at least have a running start.

One of the things I want to leave you goes beyond the inheritance of substance. It is even greater than the giving of land and bequeathing of property. It is the sharing of wisdom. Part of what a good father provides to his offspring is wisdom. Many fathers talk to their sons but say nothing to their daughters. I want my sons and daughters to impact their generations, and you cannot do that sleeping in a box under a bridge, singing hymns. You may still get to heaven, but you will have a terrible time on the trip!

Many great Christians of former generations thought speaking of financial things was carnal. That was a great message when they were young. But when they were old and saddled with medical bills and children who could not afford to care for themselves, much less their aged parents, it was evident that they failed to watch the ant and came to be in want! That's what I want you to do — watch the ant. I will discuss more about her later. She is a wise teacher.

It is not carnal to discuss money. It is part of your heritage as a Christian. The Father is like me in this regard: He wants to see you blessed. Please don't allow anyone to tell you that being a Christian means you must be poor. God doesn't mind you having money. He minds money having you. Solomon wrote that "money answereth all things" (Eccl. 10:19, KJV). It is not the answer to spirituality and eternal life. But it is the answer to all "things." I want to leave you with a few answers. Too often I see many children who are left with all the questions of life. How am I going to make it, or how am I going to pay for that? Those

are the questions, but I want you to have at least enough answers to respond to the questions of life.

While it is true that you can never trust in riches, it does not negate the fact that God is a provider, and He is not offended by good provisions. It is important that we trust in the Provider and not the provisions. Where you place your trust determines whether you can handle wealth or not. It is one thing to have it and quite another to count on it. One illness or accident can deplete all that we have. One long-term injury can change life as we know it. Jobs end and companies close. Stocks fall and investments fail. That doesn't mean you should avoid investing, working or doing whatever you can to be a wise steward of the gift of life. It does mean that after you have done all of the wise things you can do, then still trust in God.

We should look upon the ant and plan for the winter as she does! After we have done all that wisdom mandates, we can trust in nothing that we have done; we must still trust only in the God who blessed us to do it! In the midst of our faith, we yet need works; faith without works is dead, being alone (James 2:26). Many intelligent people have walked away from our faith. It wasn't because our faith was poor but because many failed to represent it correctly. What they taught as faith was foolishness. It led them to think that in order to be a Christian you had to have few goals and ambitions. They thought we were people who walked around with our eyes to the skies waiting for our Lord without affecting our world. That is not the truth.

> Go to the ant, thou sluggard; consider her ways, and be wise: Which having no guide, overseer, or ruler, provideth her meat in the summer, and gathereth her food in the harvest (Prov. 6:6-8, KJV).

The ant teaches us to be good investors and not just consumers. Most of us spend all of our income on looking

prosperous. It is like spending all of the money for your house on drapes without windows, or carpeting without floors. What good is a beautiful wall without a foundation? Investing is hard for carnal Christians because carnal people always love to see everything. In order to be an investor, you have to have a propensity for delayed gratification.

This is the time of opportunity. God is setting up a window, particularly for His daughters who were once economically oppressed by bigoted thinking that did not want women to have finances, because money would empower them to make choices. Poverty is a silent prison. It has no walls, and it needs no chains. It restrains us with limited options and loss of hope. Its jailer is despair, and its guards are depression. Flee from it! You are the daughters of a rich man. You are the daughters of God! Don't just dress like the wealthy (who, incidentally, seldom dress well). But secure your future.

Your income-yielding years are limited. You must move while you can — like the wise ant who worked through the summer and then was able to laugh at the winter. Believe me, many elderly women are not laughing at the winter. The cold blight of age and lost income have left their arthritic knees too stiff to bend for fervent prayer. They are in trouble. The Bible speaks to the sluggard, but it is not always laziness that ensnares. Many times it is poor planning and misguided spirituality that caused many men and women to be left depleted. Many have allowed themselves to be prostituted while others were empowered because of them. But they themselves were left depleted and depressed.

I want to give you a few pearls of wisdom, coupled with whatever inheritance I can muster, to prepare you for days when I cannot reach you. What I have bequeathed to you will make my memory far more meaningful. They are simple biblical truths that will assist you in reaching goals

and aspirations. They will be beneficial to you as a woman, because men have a tendency to deal with tangibles whereas some women lean toward abstractions.

I will explain. My wife loves greeting cards. She will weep over a card. I can give her an expensive coat, and she will weep over the card. She has matches from the restaurant where we had our first date. She has towels — oops — I mean napkins from the honeymoon suite! She has memorabilia that is absolutely worthless to anyone else but her. These things are treasures to her. Now I appreciate a good card — don't get me wrong. But if anyone wants to get me an expensive gift, don't be upset if you can't get it wrapped or find a card. Put it in a paper sack and write my name in crayon. It will be just fine with me.

I am not saying my wife is wrong. We respect and even celebrate our differences. I never criticize people for being themselves. I am merely pointing out the great difference in our perspective. Men generally give *things* more easily than we give affections. We feel safer giving tangibles, whereas most women want men to give of themselves, which is, by the way, terrifying to most men.

Because men put so much value on things, they have monopolized the market on industry and commerce and have many times locked out women who would aspire to operate on another level. Successful men understand money to be power and symbolic of control.

Unfortunately, we are living in an age when the number of single parents is on the rise, and for various reasons many women are finding themselves in need of tangibles. They are dressing in business suits and saying to corporate America, Scoot over and make room! The church, which tends to run a beat behind on social issues, is waking up also. No longer are saved women content to bake pies and cookies while the men buy yachts and play golf. God is

raising up women who can be decisive and effective in a board room and still be feminine and sensitive in the bedroom! You can have a career, goals and aspirations and still be a good mother or a good wife.

Nevertheless, we have been delinquent in preaching this truth. The Bible wasn't delinquent about declaring it. In the tradition and power of *Woman, Thou Art Loosed!*, I want to share a few steps that may help the woman who has been sluggish, if not a sluggard, to better prepare for the future and make better choices!

1. Preparation and Presentation of Your Request

> Our father died in the wilderness, and he was not in the company of them that gathered themselves together against the Lord in the company of Korah; but died in his own sin, and had no sons. Why should the name of our father be done away from among his family, because he hath no son? Give unto us therefore a possession among the brethren of our father (Num. 27:3-4, KJV).

These women came to Moses and began to negotiate for betterment. They didn't go into a rage of emotions. They approached Moses with undeniable facts. They were not impulsive. They took the time to prepare, and they laid out a case for which they had to be respected. They articulated it powerfully.

You can never receive anything without being a person who knows how to ask. That means you can't sit there and stew until you are hysterical, and then have a screaming fit at someone in authority. If you alienate the one you have to ask, you have disassociated yourself from the solution, and you are left with the problem.

The responsibility of initiation rests on you. You must

142

be an initiator of the blessing, but be sure that you come with the facts and lay them out in a systematic, coherent order. Never allow the enemy to use your emotions against you!

If you never ask for anything, you will never receive anything; the world will assume you are satisfied. Passivity will block you from receiving. Many people are so passive that they hang around life as limp as old rag dolls and never stand up to circumstances or enforce change. They are waiting for a prince to rescue them. The other extreme is the people who argue about everything. They are bitter and mean, priding themselves on being overbearing and outspoken.

Neither person is effective. Overbearing women end their lives in isolation. They are isolated because men find them so obnoxious that they would rather bypass them than confront them. The other type, Sis. Rag Doll, is taken for granted and abused because she never speaks out against injustice; she feels powerless to provoke change. These women that the Bible is speaking about were women who would speak up without ranting and raving. The trick is to be balanced between two extremes.

> It is better to dwell in a corner of the housetop, than with a brawling woman in a wide house (Prov. 21:9, KJV).

However, even God will not release blessings to someone who will not speak up. He teaches emphatically the necessity of being an initiator. You must initiate your own blessing. If you don't initiate it, nothing significant will ever occur in your life. It is totally up to you.

> Ask, and it shall be given you; seek, and ye shall find; knock, and it shall be opened unto you (Matt. 7:7, KJV).

If there is no asking, seeking and knocking, there will be no giving, finding and opening. Can you see why many women are living in frustration? They are filled with many wonderful memories and fantasies, but their reality may not be what they desire.

These women went to Moses. They didn't wait on Moses to come to them. When they went, they were initiating a change. Sometimes it may be difficult to see yourself as an initiator, but if you don't prepare and present yourself correctly, you are going to be stagnant and miserable.

Too many people sit around and wish something would happen. If you have dreams and aspirations, you must be confident in what you feel and move toward those goals with vigor and precision. Most Christians feel that God will do it all. That is not true. If Hannah had not prayed in the spirit for a child (faith) and then slept with Elkanah (works), there would have never been a Samuel (fruit) (1 Sam. 1:20).

You have to make your actions line up with your convictions, or you will live a fruitless life. What is even worse is the fact that in your old age you will have to eat the fruit of what you did with your youth. Be careful what you cook!

2. Right Must Challenge Wrong

"Why should the name of our father disappear just because he had no son? We feel that we should be given property along with our father's brothers" (Num. 27:4, TLB).

It is said that this is a man's world. It is not a man's world; it is God's world. He is the only sovereign power. Men may be occupying many seats of authority, but God is in control. If He blesses you, do not fear. A blessed woman can survive even in a man's world. The challenge is to receive what is yours without becoming bitter about the

times it was withheld from you. Bitterness is counterproductive and will stop you from enjoying the victory, even if you get it. Many people are so full of anger that they cannot enjoy what they have attained because they harbor so much resentment and repressed anger.

Unfortunately, many sectors of our society still maintain various degrees of racism and sexism. It is tragic that in our modern societies there are still those who, purely on the basis of superficial externals, have alienated and discriminated against people who are equally God's children. These voices that would limit persons from the pursuit of their dreams should be challenged. It is imperative that their ignorance not be allowed to build a prison within which you have to live.

The truth is that a woman's place is where she finds it. Not all are meant to be mothers. Not all women are domestic. Some may be able to balance both roles; others may have a definite direction they want to choose. God is not offended by your aspirations. He is not intimidated by your pursuit. While some reach into the heavens for all that life has to offer, others prefer quiet contentment and tranquility. If a woman is satisfied to live at a certain economic level, that is her right, regardless of whether it is very high or very low.

We all make choices. Some very vibrant and intelligent women trade fame and fortune for peace and quiet. It is a matter of preference. Do not allow peer pressure to force you into a role that makes you uncomfortable. Our right, as God's children, is to press toward goals and promises that are as unique and diverse as we are ourselves. Even animals have a strategy for the future. It is crucial that you also prepare a strategy by assessing the environment in which you must survive and begin to make preparations for the changing seasons of life. If the ant has to do it, then so do you.

The daughter who aspires to a lofty goal that she is capable of managing emotionally and academically should not be restricted purely on the basis of gender. Neither should other women try to belittle her because she has chosen to express her gifting in an arena that may not be seen by society as traditional. Need I remind you that the virtuous woman in Proverbs 31 was a businesswoman who owned property, produced products, sold goods and cared for her family? She was a woman of the nineties. Do not allow even well-meaning Christians to box you in with their personal preferences. A single woman is submitted to her God. A married woman is submitted to her husband.

> It is the same with a girl who marries. She faces the same problem. A girl who is not married is anxious to please the Lord in all she is and does. But a married woman must consider other things such as housekeeping and the likes and dislikes of her husband. I am saying this to help you (1 Cor. 7:34-35, TLB).

Beyond the submission outlined in Scripture, tell everyone else to stop playing God with your future. In spiritual matters, whether you are married or unmarried, submit to your pastor (Heb. 13:17). Let's look back again at these precious daughters of Zelophehad who went to Moses to challenge the fairness of the "good ol' boys" policy that was in effect. Their actions suggested, "We are women, but we are blessed women." In other words, we are not cursed, and we have the right to walk as any other blessed person walks. They did it without male bashing or disrespect to authority. They went through proper channels, but bless God, they went through. You don't want to be rebellious, because rebellion is as the sin of witchcraft (1 Sam. 15:23). Nevertheless, you still want to get what the Father has for you to inherit. They did not want to be

excluded on the basis of their gender. Do you?

If you are going to be effective in this age, you must know that you have a right to be blessed. In fact, our ability is proof of our rights. The very fact that God has endowed you with ability is, in fact, indicative of the fact that He has a purpose for you. If He gave you the gifting, you will have to give an account of what you did with what He gave you.

I believe that every day is a gift from God. What you do with that day or talent is, in fact, your gift to Him. Have you hidden your talent because you ran into opposition and someone said you didn't have it? Did they say it was because you are a woman? That is ridiculous. You are only limited by your own mind's creativity and concentration.

> Then he which had received the one talent came and said, Lord, I knew thee that thou art an hard man, reaping where thou hast not sown, and gathering where thou hast not strawed: And I was afraid, and went and hid thy talent in the earth: lo, there thou hast that is thine. His lord answered and said unto him, Thou wicked and slothful servant, thou knewest that I reap where I sowed not, and gather where I have not strawed (Matt. 25:24-26, KJV).

Many women have suppressed their God-given ability in order to live up to some negative stereotype. It is that same stereotype God wants them to shatter. You have neglected a right that the Father made great sacrifices to give you! What a price He has paid to give you your inheritance! It cost the Father His Son's life. It is comparable to me as a natural father working all of my life to give you, as my daughter, my inheritance, and then you squander what I have worked to provide. Or worse still, you refuse to claim it because you are a woman.

147

These women challenged the system. They challenged it at a time when women were considered second-class citizens. In spite of public opinion, they chose to challenge and speak up for their rights, and they got what they fought to attain. Many of you are dying from apathy and boredom. You have not challenged life, and you are not being challenged by life. You need to exercise your potential.

Get your blood circulating. Good, spiritual aerobic exercise would start your heart pumping vitality and stimulation. You need more life in your life. A challenging life can even help keep us from mischief and sin. When we are bored, Satan takes the initiative. You know where that leads.

One of the challenges was a challenge in their own mind. We are limited by our own tendency to settle for less than what we could attain. If you are not careful, you will talk yourself out of living. The challenged mind will speak up and it will say to others, I need more life in my life. The daughters of Zelophehad simply refused to be wallflowers when they had the Father's favor.

3. The Father's Favor

They were not disrespectful or rude. They just dared to disagree with the conditions that oppressed them. Something within them felt they were justified. It is easier to fight when right is on your side. Always be sure you are right. When right is on your side, then God is on your side. One of the greatest tools you can use in a battle is the blessed assurance that you are right.

God is righteous, and when all is said and done, He is for the right. If you are right, you can be as still or as small as you please. But I dare you to be right. If you are right, when all is said and done, you will arise victorious. Never go to battle out of flesh or pride — the greater part of your strength is in being right. How could God bless wrong?

That's what separates faith from humanism. Humanism

teaches the power of the human spirit. It basically suggests that if you believe anything hard enough, you can make it come to pass. Faith, on the other hand, empowers you to attain what the Father has promised. It is hinged on the Father's Word. Without the human spirit being nailed to the Father's will, we would have pure witchcraft. Manipulation would take over our hearts. Women would be pressing husbands to leave their wives. It would be chaos. God only enables you to do what He has ordained you to do. You don't want the power to do wrong.

Why would you want the power to attain the blessing that is intended for someone else? You just want what is yours. If that is not the case, you had better stop now and begin to pray until your desires have been bathed in His Word and your motives become godly. If you are wrestling with a need to control other people and are trying to influence their will with yours, you may not know it, but you are wrestling with the spirit of witchcraft! It must be renounced. That is not a spirit to be played with. You would be surprised at the people who are overcome with a need to control things that are not theirs.

> "Why should the name of our father disappear just because he had no son? We feel that we should be given property along with our father's brothers" (Num. 27:4, TLB).

Notice that these women asked for their portion. They didn't want their uncle's portion. They just wanted what was rightfully theirs. They wanted property "along with" their father's brothers. They were aggressive enough to see it, but they were not lawless — they requested it. They were not male bashers. Christian women must avoid taking their cue from their secular sisters who have not allowed their bitter experiences to be healed by the love of our Father, who takes the sting out of life's traumas.

The daughters of Zelophehad never lost their femininity. There is a difference between femininity and timidity. They didn't tolerate injustice, nor did they become embittered. It is the power of a request! I know it is difficult to be ignored and not become disgruntled. But remember that wise women — in fact, wise people period — do not allow their emotions to overrule their ultimate goals and purpose.

Because these women challenged the system without violating the principles, Moses went back to God and asked Him for direction. There are some systems that have ensnared your blessing. They need to be challenged but not attacked. I sense this as a time when God wants to literally pour out blessings, not just to His sons, but also to His daughters. This is more than an extra check in the mail. It is time for directional changes and life changes. I want you to start expecting a deluge, an outpouring. I don't mean just wait on it. No, prepare for it and expect it. It is going to rain in your life. That is why He wants to heal every fear and insecurity and inhibition that would stop you. This blessing must be provoked, but when it comes it will rain.

> And on my servants and on my handmaidens I will pour out in those days of my Spirit; and they shall prophesy (Acts 2:18, KJV).

God has always had an equal bill of rights for His people. There is no difference between what He will pour out on His sons and what He will pour out on His daughters. He is a good Father. It is His will to bless you. Can you agree with God right now for the returning flow of creative, unrestricted prosperity in every area of your life? This is a wake-up call for you. The time is right, and the procedure must be right. The Father is going to shake up the powers that have held your blessing.

I am writing with a strong feeling of release in my spirit. The Father wants to release the held-up blessing to the

pressed-down daughter. You see, ultimately the Father's will is what matters. That is what will be done. So Moses asked the Father about their Father's will!

> And Moses brought their cause before the Lord. And the Lord spake unto Moses, saying, The daughters of Zelophehad speak right: thou shalt surely give them a possession of an inheritance among their father's brethren; and thou shalt cause the inheritance of their father to pass unto them. And thou shalt speak unto the children of Israel, saying, If a man die, and have no son, then ye shall cause his inheritance to pass unto his daughter (Num. 27:5-8, KJV).

If you have the favor of your Father, no one can stop you from being blessed. It is important that you don't waste strength fighting the opposition. You see, if God is for you, who can be against you (Rom. 8:31)? You have the favor from God. Don't worry about who is against you, just keep thinking about who is for you. Your faith will be built through conflict and peril.

This was the first case of gender discrimination mentioned in the Scriptures. And the court of heaven ruled in the favor of some women who knew how to go after what their father had in his estate! Perhaps there are some things that your father has for you. Do not be intimidated. You may be a single parent. There may not be a "son" to fend for you. Your husband may be long gone. Your blessing doesn't center around a man or men in general. In spite of what you don't have, look at what you do have and keep on walking. By God's grace and power you can still receive the inheritance.

Let me explain. As a father, I need to know that I have prepared for my children's today and their tomorrow. I can sleep better if I have some assurance that, if I would slip

away and be at rest, I have left provision for my family. I would be angry to think that I had left an inheritance for my daughters and they were living in poverty. I worked hard to be sure they would have advantages.

> If ye then, being evil, know how to give good gifts unto your children, how much more shall your Father which is in heaven give good things to them that ask him? (Matt. 7:11, KJV)

He is a better father than I am. Why don't you as a woman of God go after what the Father has willed to you? He died for you, and He wants you to have your inheritance. Every time you experience one of His benefits, thank Him, because if He hadn't willed it, well, it just wouldn't be yours. I encourage you as a father would his daughter, go for all that life has to offer you. Take a large slice of life. Savor every bite. Your Father has willed you good things.

If you have been walking around with a drab spirit and a broken heart, I am talking to you. If you have been in a state of depression that is robbing you of these precious years when you should be thriving and in pursuit of destiny, hear this word. Don't spend another day wasted in regret, sleeping away your mercy and losing your chance to achieve. Get up and get busy. You may have to work it out. You may have to push and shove. But life is worth the struggle. Now pull off those ragged house shoes and that gingham dress. Take those curlers out of your hair. Take a long, hot, luxurious bath and put on some sweet cologne. If you want it, you can have it. Your Father left you loaded!

Chapter Twelve

Talitha Cumi —
Damsel, Arise!

In the flickering, candle-like glow that quietly christens the room of a treasured soul, there — wrapped in footie pajamas and surrounded by doll babies and teddy bears — lies your mother's joy and your father's heart. The tender light will burn through the night to remind you that your safety is our first concern. Now whispered prayers and gentle hugs add spice to the room, and the sounds of love fill the air.

Daughters, whose bright eyes and burning hearts promise

153

to shake nations and capture the hearts of many men, run from the suitors and walk with the Savior. He will not fail you. You went from diapers to training pants. You moved from frilly lace Easter dresses to silk purses and black pumps. Just imagine, my babies making oatmeal, cooking breakfast, feeding others, touching the world. You are the stardust of my dreams and the answer to your mother's prayers. You will have days that are brighter than mine and moments that are richer than my wildest hopes. Look for them, expect them, and if they don't come, make them happen. Insist on taking a bite out of life and touching heaven. It is your right. You are the daughter of a king.

You are greater than the repercussions of your past. You are stronger than a moment of failure. You can rise like smoke up a chimney. You were meant to spiral to the sky. All the chilling drafts of broken promises should not deny you the gift of life. Never forget you are alive — sometimes weak, sometimes strong, but nevertheless alive. You will be right some days and wrong some nights, but don't stop waking up in the morning. The morning is God giving you another chance to pass the exam. He is giving you a chance to benefit from faults and fight forward.

> Kiss me again and again, for your love is sweeter than wine (Song 1:2, TLB).

He has kissed you gently, tenderly, but definitely. It is not the urgent kiss of a desperate lover who makes demands in the night. He has kissed you with the gentle kiss of a Father's favor whose tenderness would shield you from the traumas of the past. You have been kissed, blessed — touched. One smooch, gently sent from heaven's lips to human pain. You are kissed by the Father Himself. No wonder Satan has failed to destroy in the night what God has prepared for the light. You have been kissed.

This is what you have to know if you are to withstand the

night. This is what you have to rehearse against the goblins of old images and past memories that would assault your dreams and turn them into nightmares. The devil is a liar. Just as sure as a father's kiss would ease a nervous child who must sleep in a strange place, this is a sedative for you. No matter how foreign this stage in your life may seem, you must know He prepared you for it. When He kissed you, He shielded you, and you are His. Safe and secure from all alarms, you are to rest in the sanctity and safety of arms that will not fail you. A kiss good night is His way of sealing you till morning. And it will come; it will not tarry. The morning is yours. Spend it well, use it sparingly. It is a gift.

I love the morning. It is for the hopeful, not the regretful. It is expectation. It is wet dew moistening dry ground. It is hummingbirds and honking horns and a city yawning into alertness. Greater still, it is the future lying naked before us. Daybreak is stretching in the fresh hours of a new opportunity just created. It is an empty tomb and a filled manger. It is life, love and hope. Never forget about the breaking of day. It will come. Nights will change, tears will dry and enemies leave. And you will come out in the morning.

If you are tired, rest in the light of these words and sleep on the cloud of His love. Don't stop moving and living. This is your day, and this is your Father's world. He has created it just for you. You are an heir to the universe. Your only boundaries are your own perceptions of potential. You can reach farther than your fingers and leap higher than your doubt. If you lift your head and raise your hands, the clouds will run away. You are kissed. Didn't you know it? Haven't you realized? That's why you are alive to show it. So show up and show off and show out. It is morning!

Never lose that little girl belief in the impossible. The fantasies of the faithful dispel the myths of the frightened.

Somebody blow me a trumpet! The races are about to begin, and the daughters of God are all dressed up. They have stripped themselves of the cares of this world. They have washed away the abuse of their childhood. They have demanded their inheritance, nursed their own babies, strengthened themselves and prepared their feet for running.

They are sisters of the cross, survivors of the secrets. They have lain awake trembling and even cried through the night. Some have screamed from bruised lips, assaulted bodies, broken hearts, betrayed trust! But what of the night? That's right, what of it? Haven't you heard? It is morning.

Tell the executive that black pumps and tweed skirts are on the elevator. They are moving from the poor house to the White House. Fresh out of fear, they are on the move.

Loosed women? You had better believe it. They are loosed from the tragedy of a long and dismal night. They are the daughters of Abraham. They are women with a promise. Precious promises are waiting for loosed women who have made themselves ready to take the kingdom by force. No more forbidden fruit for them; they are taking a bite out of life. No more restrictions or inhibitions. Many have been held back by the fear of failure and rejection. Tell the critics the Father says, "Let My daughter go!" Only a foolish man would fight a man for his daughter. It is the Father that they will have to fight. You are loosed! Run!

> And this woman, a daughter of Abraham as she is,
> whom Satan has bound for eighteen long years,
> should she not have been released from this bond
> on the Sabbath day? (Luke 13:16, NAS).

Don't look back or around or over. This is your time. It is your moment. This is the hour; God has been waiting to do for you. You have been released. It is morning. The

night is past. The fear subsides; the victim trembles, but she survives. Why shouldn't you be loosed? You can't change where you've been, but you can change where you are going.

This is the truth: I have a friend, and He is for you. Let me tell you about your father's Friend. He is stronger than I. He is strength. I have saved this moment to tell you all He will do, because you know how squeamish fathers can be when talking about intimacy and love. Well, I saved it for last.

I know there will be pain that will try to rob the passion that God created for you and your husband to enjoy. Satan is the one who will try to destroy your marriage through stress and unforgiveness. He will try to callous your soft, supple flesh and leave you with a hard shell that imprisons a broken heart. He will allow you to worship and sing, but he is afraid for you to love and give. There is a level of romance and chivalry that the Father meant for you to enjoy, not just sex but sensitivity. More than performance, I am talking to you about the return of passion.

If you are not careful, life will cause you to leak. Your marriage will become drained by the leaking passion and wilted excitement that hard times and struggles produce. Your mommyhood will try to rob you of your womanhood. Satan wants to leave you drab and aloof, hiding behind religious excuses rather than fighting your way out and being the wife and the woman you were created to be.

Perhaps you do not need this now. Perhaps it seems needless and irrelevant. But someday when you feel a heavy depression about to trample on what was once a vibrant love, you will need to turn to your father's Friend. When that day comes, suddenly you realize your husband is longing for the woman that you used to be, could be or wanted to be. Somewhere beneath your problems there is another woman screaming, Let me out! I want to love and

live. This is the woman who has been starved beneath low self-esteem and fear of rejection. She is the woman you were before. Remember her?

She is soft and sensitive, fanciful and frilly. She is bright-eyed and full of mischief, creative and sensual. Your husband has been on a fast, waiting for her to step out of the freezer. If ever there were a time that you needed to stop suppressing her and let her loose, it is now.

Who could plow through the scabs and scars in your life but Jesus? Once He does, He leaves no telltale traces, no cold attitudes as a memorial to the past. It is morning! You will never fall into that sleepy, lethargic state of melancholy depression again! Get up now.

I can't leave you lying in the bed of despair. Your emotions are dead, your passion subdued, your attitude cynical, your disposition critical. God said, Arise. You are about to have a resurrection. It will be so strong that your husband should feel it. Your children should feel it. Yes, from the prayer room to the bedroom, a loosed woman is free!

True spirituality is not at the expense of humanity. God graces the married to taste the fruit of their relationship in a unique way. He wants you to be creative. Many women, in an attempt to be more spiritual, have suppressed the anointing oil of their marriage, and it's dry! Uncap the oil, and anoint the feet of the one whom God has entrusted to your care. No one should be more glad to see you loosed!

> There is difference also between a wife and a virgin. The unmarried woman careth for the things of the Lord, that she may be holy both in body and in spirit: but she that is married careth for the things of the world, how she may please her husband (1 Cor. 7:34, KJV).

The married woman "careth for the things of the world." She is creative and resourceful, not so heavenly minded that

she is no earthly good. She is not repressed and insecure. She is loosed. I hope he's ready — she is creative. He should also be attentive and vibrant. She is full of ideas that are exciting and fresh. You have been through a metamorphosis that ought to positively affect every area of your life. Woman, thou art loosed!

> And he cometh to the house of the ruler of the synagogue, and seeth the tumult, and them that wept and wailed greatly. And when he was come in, he saith unto them, Why make ye this ado, and weep? The damsel is not dead, but sleepeth. And they laughed him to scorn. But when he had put them all out, he taketh the father and the mother of the damsel, and them that were with him, and entereth in where the damsel was lying. And he took the damsel by the hand, and said unto her, Talitha cumi; which is, being interpreted, Damsel, I say unto thee, arise. And straightway the damsel arose, and walked; for she was of the age of twelve years. And they were astonished with a great astonishment (Mark 5:38-42, KJV).

In the true tradition of ancient chivalry, where there were princes, drawbridges, damsels in distress and villains in pursuit, Jairus, the ruler of the synagogue, sent for Jesus because his daughter was sick. By the time Jesus had healed the woman with the issue of blood, Jairus' daughter had succumbed to her affliction. She was laid on a bed in the upper chamber, and neighbors came to mourn the passing of a dear damsel.

None could reverse her dismal fate. The whole family dissolved in tears; hope was gone. Perhaps some have gathered around you to weep and mourn, thinking your life is over. Some may think that your love is over, that your creativity and passion have succumbed to some emotional or

spiritual affliction with which you were wrestling. But, my daughter, Jairus' friend would not allow them to commit her to the ground. He came for her. He came with all the gallantry of a prince. He came with the courage of a mighty man destined to save a damsel in distress.

His shiny armor was the glory of the Lord. His sword was in His mouth. He came in the room and put the doubters out. There can be no doubter crying in your ear, not when you are trying to resurrect your relationship, not when you are trying to revive a part of you that Satan is trying to steal. You can't use your relationship with God to stay in a state of denial. If something has gone out of your life and your heart, we must believe God for its return.

Just when they thought she would not come back, there came Jesus. Likewise, just when others have decided you won't be back, here He comes. He comes into your life like a medieval prince, clad in righteousness, dipped in blood. He comes to heal and restore your faith and expectation, your romance and tenderness. If life has left you disenchanted and aloof, remember He is your knight in shining armor. Do not allow the vicious bandits of misfortune and abuse to rob you of your enthusiasm and vigor for life.

Many women have been through so much that they exist like empty houses on crowded streets. They are standing amid the activity of life, but there is no light in them. Oh, yes, their exteriors are beautiful, but there is a strange feeling of vacancy that hinders real beauty from shining through. Some may not notice, but under close scrutiny a discerning eye cannot help but view evidences of a deserted heart and a forsaken smile.

It is to these haunted houses that I write. These are the women whose lives have ceased to celebrate. They have lost the iridescent shimmer that would suggest life and love. They have ceased from lovemaking and life-making. They are just holding on. They have fallen into the lethargic

sleep of those who expect no company. Touch yourself and know in your heart, Jesus is coming!

Some would say, I am too old. Others would say, It is too late. Some would say, I am too busy. Some would even dare to suggest that they are too spiritual. But I declare to you that when God kissed the first lump of clay and breathed into that muddy shell the breath of life, He spoke life, and the abstract became vibrant and alive. The Master's kiss turned a ceramic into a personality. He breathed upon the vessel, and in one breath He blew blood and bone, thought and idea, attraction and affection, romance and revival. He blew so hard that He blew reproduction into the frame. He blew generations of destiny into Adam. You and I are still sucking in that breath and feeling it flood our frame with life. We are alive, the greatest computer ever witnessed. What a kiss!

These are the lips of a loving Master whose caress rebukes death. The same lips that blew upon the clay spoke to the daughter of Jairus, the ruler of the synagogue. I call Him my friend. He is the Friend of every father who has a daughter he loves and yet cannot always affect. He can do what men cannot do. He can resurrect the cold places in the heart of the woman whose love and life have been rocked to sleep in a cradle of despair. I commend you — and all the women of the world who have ever fallen asleep in the middle of life — to Him.

The bed cannot hold you — the morning has come. It is the time for arousing the apathetic. That is what revival really is. It is more than a long meeting in a crowded church. People can meet for weeks and not experience revival. Revival occurs when that which was dead is revived. It is the waking up of the cast down. You can have a revival in your spiritual life, your personal life, your financial life or whatever part of you the enemy has rocked to sleep. Just call on the Prince of Peace. His name is Jesus. He

is your father's friend. He will be there for you when I am long gone.

He is the Prince who revives what life has extinguished. His kiss can wake up the sleeping beauty. One kiss from Him can restore every area of your life, both natural and spiritual. He is the One who can walk in the room and speak to the romance that the enemy is trying to kill. He says, Damsel, arise!

If you are in a catatonic state, everyone with whom you are associated is affected. You see, the whole family is waiting. Husbands are living with the ghost of what you would have been, should have been and were meant to be. But there is another woman in you. She is neither timid nor afraid. She is not angry or insecure — she is whole. It is she who must be awakened. There is another wife in you, a gentler, softer, more loving, more giving wife who has been repressed by circumstances.

But this is not just for the benefit of others. It is for your benefit. You need to be loosed and free. There is another woman who has a key to your destiny. She is courageous and resilient, determined and assertive. The Word awakens that which should have been awake and puts to sleep some of the issues that should have retired a long time ago. This is the announcement that your soul has been waiting for. This is the announcement that releases you from the long night of repression and guilt. This is the announcement that the nation will feel. It is the blaring sound of an alarm clock shaking with the intensity of its convictions.

> And that, knowing the time, that now it is high time to awake out of sleep: for now is our salvation nearer than when we believed. The night is far spent, the day is at hand: let us therefore cast off the works of darkness, and let us put on the armour of light (Rom. 13:11-12, KJV).

To all of you who almost overslept, to all of you who have shed tears and thought you missed your chance, to all of you who ever felt that you were too deeply entrenched, to the damsel whose hair has grayed and steps have tempered, to the college student whose willowy arms are full of books and whose heart is full of questions, to all lovely damsels, young and old, black and white, simply said, but firmly meant, *Talitha cumi!* It is morning!

Epilogue

Signing Off

Dear Daughters of the Father,

I have written a word from the Father. It is His word whether you are the daughter of a president or the daughter of an accident. He loves you just the same.

I want my daughters to peek beneath the clay shell that I am encased in and inspect the inner aspects of my heart for them. I feel that I have purchased insurance, insurance that time will never erase the testimony that I want to always be alive for them and their children. It is a testament of my intentions toward them and my intense love for our Father.

I also want you to have a glimpse of the heart of an earthly father whose frailties and humanity are daily strengthened by a heavenly Father. I know there are many women across this land whose hearts have been broken by the lack of a father. Some have been torn by the hands of the father they had. I am sorry. Yet we cannot stay there. Beyond yesterday's night there is tomorrow's morning. It is truly morning for those women who have given their hearts to Jesus. If you haven't given your heart to Him, please do it now. He is so much help for those who need a touch.

If something in your heart turns over whenever you see a father holding a child, or you see an older man walking with his daughter in the park, and miss the father that slipped away from you, be encouraged. You are not alone. Your Father is higher than the stars and yet closer than breath, and He sent me to tell women of all ages and stages to come, come and sit safely on the lap of His love. No matter how you have suffered or what you have endured, there is something He wants you to know. Without a doubt, Daddy loves His girls.

Love ♥ always,

Daddy

Other Books by T. D. Jakes

Woman, Thou Art Loosed!

Can You Stand to Be Blessed?

Water in the Wilderness

Why?

Naked and Not Ashamed

Loose That Man and Let Him Go!

Video Packages by T. D. Jakes

MANPOWER I: Healing the Wounded Man Within

MANPOWER II

Marriage: Bonding or Binding

Forgiveness: Final Frontier

Make This House a Home

For more information on tapes, books and
other products, please write or call:

Jakes Ministries
P.O. Box 7056
Charleston, WV 25356
1-800-BISHOP-2